The Heinle

PICTURE DICTIONARY

for Children

HEINLE
CENGAGE Learning

Australia • Brazil • Japan • Korea • Mexico • Singapore • Spain • United Kingdom • United States

HEINLE
CENGAGE Learning

**The Heinle Picture Dictionary
for Children**
Jill Korey O'Sullivan

Publisher: Sherrise Roehr

Director of Content Development:
Anita Raducanu

Development Editor: John Hicks

Editorial Assistant: Katherine Reilly

Director of Product Marketing:
Amy T. Mabley

Executive Marketing Manager:
Jim McDonough

Product Marketing Manager: Katie Kelley

International Marketing Manager:
Ian Martin

Senior Content Project Manager:
Maryellen Killeen

Content Project Manager:
Dawn Marie Elwell

Asset Development Coordinator:
Noah Vincelette

Associate Media Development Editor:
Jonelle Lonergan

Senior Print Buyer: Mary Beth Hennebury

Indexer: Alexandra Nickerson

Project Management and Composition:
InContext Publishing Partners

Interior Designer: Dawn Marie Elwell

Cover Designers: Studio Montage and
Dawn Marie Elwell

Credits appear on page 148, which constitutes
a continuation of the copyright page.

Student Edition (hardcover)
ISBN-10: 1-4240-0711-9
ISBN-13: 978-1-4130-2256-8

Student Edition (softcover)
ISBN-10: 1-4130-2256-1
ISBN-13: 978-1-4240-0711-0

International Student Edition (softcover)
ISBN-10: 1-4240-0460-8
ISBN-13: 978-1-4240-0460-7
(Not for Sale in the United States)

Library of Congress Control Number: 2007922762

Heinle
25 Thomson Place
Boston, MA 02210
USA

Cengage Learning is a leading provider of customized learning solutions with office locations around the globe, including Singapore, the United Kingdom, Australia, Mexico, Brazil and Japan. Locate our local office at:
international.cengage.com/region

Cengage Learning products are represented in Canada by Nelson Education, Ltd.

Visit Heinle online at **elt.heinle.com**
Visit our corporate website at **cengage.com**

Printed in China
3 4 5 6 7 8 9 10   11 10 09 08

Contents at a Glance

Contents

Acknowledgments

Many thanks to the Heinle team, with special thanks to Sherrise Roehr and John Hicks for their great dedication and imagination.

For my dear, sweet Anna, whose second word (after "quack") was "book" and whose favorite book is the dictionary.

-- Jill Korey O'Sullivan

The publisher would like to thank the following reviewers and focus group participants:

Erin Anguilano
Bennett Elementary
Ft. Lauderdale, FL

Kristi T. Arriaga
West Lake Year Round Elementary
Apex, NC

Cecilia Avila Portuanto
University of Xalapa;
University of Ameicana Latina
Xalapa, Mexico

Linda Beesley
Clark County School District
Las Vegas, NV

Laura Bowkley
EC London
London, United Kingdom

Kathryn Brennan
Boston Renaissance Charter
   Public School
Boston, MA

Tim Budden
Taipei European School
   British Section
Taipei, Taiwan

Christine Coombe
Dubai Men's College
Dubai, United Arab Emirates

Philip Anthony Drury
Ist. Maria Ausiliatrice
Caltagirone, Italy

Dianne Elkins
PISD Thomas Elementary ESL
Plano, TX

Kristen Eschmann
Stoklasa Middle School
Lowell, MA

Luz Fox
Thiriot Elementary
Las Vegas, NV

Carmen Goheen
Jerry Thomas Elementary
Jupiter, FL

Ana Rosa Solórzano Gowman
Guadalajara, Mexico

Jennifer Gracey
Berlitz Japan, Inc.

Maria Hetu
Plymouth Public Schools
Plymouth, MA

Beatriz Iglesias
EIDE
Bizkaia, Spain

Melissa Jones
Palmetto Elementary
West Palm Beach, FL

Fergal Kavanagh
Napoli, Italy

Mary Kessing
Creative Corner Children's Center
Winchester, MA

Kevin Kornburger
Kanda University of International
   Studies
Chiba-ken, Japan

Carolyn Krack
Jo Mackey Elementary
North Las Vegas, NV

Megan LaVogue
Jupiter Elementary
Palm Beach, FL

Helen le Port
IFG Langues
Puteaux, France

Adilen Lucal
Belvedere Elementary
West Palm Beach, FL

Kevin Miller
Kailua-Kona, HI

Carolyn Odenwelder
Brassfield Elementary
Raleigh, NC

Belgin Öðrek
Florya Koleji
Istanbul, Turkey

Brendan Ó Sé
UCC Ireland
Cork, Ireland

Mae-Ran Park
Pukyong National University
Korea

Maria Luiza Vieira Pedrosa
Belo Horizonte, Brazil

Edgar Arruda Pimentel
MAI English Schools
Belo Horizonte, Brazil

Claudia Sasía Pinzón
Instituto México de Puebla, AC
Cholula, Mexico

Maria-Magdalena Plawecka
I Liceum Ogólnokształcące
Jaworzno, Poland

Dana C. Powers
Jo Mackey Elementary
North Las Vegas, NV

William Reilly
Rosa Parks Learning Center
North Hills, CA

Karin Rich
Elaine Wynn Elementary School
Las Vegas, NV

Wayne Rimmer
BKC-International House Moscow
Moscow, Russia

Lupe Robles
Pearson Elementary
Modesto, CA

Waltraud M. Roithmeier
Karolinen-Gymnasium Rosenheim
Rosenheim, Germany

Adelina Ruiz
SIGNOS
Guadalajara, Mexico

Daniela R. Sandoval
Tony Alamo Elementary
Las Vegas, NV

Scott Smith
Hongik University
Seoul, Korea

Trevor Sowerby
Manchester School-Idiomas
Gijón, Spain

Wendy Superfine
The Lake School Oxford
Oxford, United Kingdom

Lale Türüt
Özel Beykent İlkögretim Okulu
Istanbul, Turkey

Deborah Wilkes
Lee Co. Schools
Sanford, NC

Lisa Young
George Washington Academy
St. George, UT

About *The Heinle Picture Dictionary for Children*

The Heinle Picture Dictionary for Children is the most powerful vocabulary builder for children learning English today. Designed to teach essential vocabulary for beginners to high beginners aged 5 to 8, *The Heinle Picture Dictionary for Children* presents words in context: *visually,* through highly colorful, realistic illustrations and photographs, and *linguistically,* through entertaining readings. Research has shown that language learners derive word meaning from context and that vocabulary is most effectively learned in context (Goerss, Beck, Mckeown, 1999; National Reading Panel, 2000). Encountering vocabulary in context enhances vocabulary development, whereas learning words in isolation results in a child's repeating only labels for words, not resulting in real language development (National Reading Panel, 2000).

With over 1,100 words, *The Heinle Picture Dictionary for Children* teaches more high-frequency English vocabulary than any other children's picture dictionary. Each of the 63 two-page lessons presents 15 to 20 words appropriate for the level and age group. Singular nouns are preceded by an indefinite article (or definite article if more natural) to help learners understand English article use, the difference between singular and plural, and the difference between count and non-count nouns. Verbs are presented either in verb-only lessons or in boxes designed to differentiate them from nouns. Adjectives and prepositions are shown in realistic contexts.

The Heinle Picture Dictionary for Children features vocabulary words in short readings related to the lesson's theme. Each lesson begins with a "Rhyme Time" or a "Fun Facts" reading. When listening to the "Rhyme Time," learners hear the pronunciation, stress, intonation, and rhythm of English. Returning to the rhyme several times builds learners' retention of target vocabulary. Rhymes engage children; promote phonemic awareness, learning, and memory; and are highly effective learning devices (Palmer, Kelley, 1992).

The "Fun Facts" readings use target vocabulary words in context with high-interest, entertaining facts about the lesson's theme. Connecting facts to vocabulary development is a strong incentive that encourages learning (Taylor, Graves, van den Broek, 2000).

Research has shown that word play activities are critical to motivate and enhance learning (Diamond, Gutlohn, 2006). It also taps into students' background knowledge so that they "connect with, make sense of, and enjoy reading" (Cohen, Kurstedt, May, 2005). The "Playing with Words" activities in *The Heinle Picture Dictionary for Children* focus on semantic understanding, phonemic awareness, and language development. They make use of three key elements of successful vocabulary development: motivating and enhancing learning (Diamond, Gutlohn, 2006); tapping

children's background knowledge to help them connect with, make sense of, and enjoy vocabulary development (Cohen, Kurstedt, May, 2005); and providing repeated and varied exposure to new words (N. Anderson, 1999).

Ideally, vocabulary development activities engage children in learning (National Reading Panel, 2000). To that end, a kid-friendly monkey is hidden in the artwork in each lesson to provide a fun warm-up activity. Young learners will enjoy locating the monkey — and engage with the dictionary pages prior to using them in class.

How to Use *The Heinle Picture Dictionary for Children*

Repeated practice with new vocabulary is essential for language learning. In addition to the activities provided in the supplements (see Support Materials), here are a few ideas that you can incorporate into the classroom.

- **Predict.** With their books closed, ask students to brainstorm words they think are related to the lesson's topic. Then have students check to see how many items they predicted correctly.

- **Assess prior knowledge.** At the beginning of the lesson, ask students to identify objects depicted in the illustrations and photographs.

- **Introduce vocabulary.** Present each word. Ask students to listen to you (or the audio) and repeat the words. Help them with pronunciation and check for comprehension. Show pictures or bring in real-life examples of the words. "Perform" verbs for the class.

- **Check comprehension.** Ask students to point to pictures that correspond to words you call out. Or, ask students to point to pictures that correspond to words embedded within a sentence or a paragraph that you read aloud.

- **Elicit additional vocabulary.** Elicit additional vocabulary related to the theme of the lesson by asking students to name other words related to the lesson's topic.

- **Play games.** For example, play Bingo with your class. Ask students to choose any five words from the dictionary lesson and write them on a piece of paper. Students check off words on their lists as you randomly call out words. The first student to check off every word on his/her list wins.

Support Materials

Research has shown that English language learners benefit from read-alouds, listening to audiotapes, activities that expand word use outside the classroom, and parent involvement (August et al., 2006). *The Heinle Picture Dictionary for Children* program contains support materials that address all learning modes — visual, auditory, and much more.

Workbook The full-color workbook is packed with fun, yet meaningful practice activities for each lesson. It targets vocabulary development, language development, phonemic awareness, and graphemic awareness.

Lesson Planner with Activity Bank CD-ROM The full-color Lesson Planner provides vocabulary development, language development, and phonics activities at three different levels for every lesson. The Activity Bank CD-ROM contains an abundance of resources to make life easier for teachers, such as:

- Activity Pages for additional vocabulary practice
- Literacy Worksheets for students new to the Roman alphabet
- Flashcards and word lists for each lesson
- "Rhyme Time," "Fun Facts," and song lyrics in a customizable format

Full-Color Transparencies Full-color transparencies contain all the artwork from the dictionary without the word labels for presenting new words and assessing vocabulary knowledge.

Classroom Presentation CD-ROM The presentation CD-ROM provides the dictionary artwork in PowerPoint format. Each lesson is available both with and without the word labels for presenting new words and assessing vocabulary knowledge.

Audio Program Audio tapes and CDs include the readings ("Rhyme Time" and "Fun Facts") as well as the target vocabulary words.

Sing-Along Audio CD 63 engaging, original songs recycle the vocabulary words presented in the dictionary.

Interactive CD-ROM Filled with engaging activities such as flashcards, matching, and spelling, the interactive CD-ROM provides fun extra practice to reinforce language skills.

To the Parent

You play a crucial role in your child's education. You can use *The Heinle Picture Dictionary for Children* at home to help your child learn English. Here are some ideas for spending time with your child and helping him or her learn English.

- **Speak and read to your child in English.** Read the new vocabulary words with your child while pointing to the pictures. Cover the word labels and ask your child, "What is this?"

- **Personalize** the new words in each lesson by asking your child to talk about his or her life in English. For example, What pets do you have? What toys do you have? What fruit do you like?

- **Point and say.** Point to items in the artwork and ask, "What's this?" Say new words and ask your child to point to them in your home or on his or her body.

- **Share.** Ask your child to say the new English words every day. Ask your child to read or retell the "Rhyme Time" or "Fun Facts" reading.

- **Draw and write.** Draw a picture of an item from your child's lesson and ask him or her to write the English word on the picture.

- **Make learning fun.** Play games with new vocabulary words. Children love to play. Play "*Simon Says*" to practice verbs. Play "*Charades*" to appeal to kinesthetic learners. Play "*Yes! or No!*" to focus on word meanings. (Make a true or false statement about one of the items. For example, "A supermarket has food" or "A bank has trains." Ask your child to tell you "Yes!" or "No!" Switch roles and ask your child to try to make the statements, while you say "Yes!" or "No!") Make it fun and encourage additional vocabulary.

Make English time a special time for you and your child. Let your child know that mistakes are OK because everyone learns from their mistakes! Most importantly, have *fun* together!

We hope *The Heinle Picture Dictionary for Children* becomes a source of engaging and meaningful language learning for your students. Please feel free to contact us at **elt.heinle.com** with your comments and suggestions.

Anderson, N. J. (1999). *Exploring second language reading: Issues and strategies.* Boston: Heinle & Heinle.

August, D., & Shanahan, T. (Eds.). (2006). Developing literacy in second-language learners: Report of the national literacy panel on language-minority children and youth. Mahwah, NJ: Lawrence Erlbaum Associates.

Cohen, Kurstedt, & May. (2005). FFF-luency and Comp-re-hension: "Making Sense" of the Reading Process. Paper presented at the Association of Childhood Education International Annual Conference, March 25, 2005.

Diamond, L., & Gutlohn, L. (2006). *Vocabulary Handbook.* Berkeley, CA: Consortium on Reading Excellence, Inc. (CORE).

Goerss, B. L., Beck, I. L., & McKeown, M. G. (1999). *Increasing Remedial Students' Ability to Derive Word Meaning from Context.* Reading Psychology, 20 (2), 151-175.

National Institute of Child Health and Human Development. (2000). *Report of the National Reading Panel. Teaching children to read: An evidence-based assessment of the scientific research literature on reading and its implications for reading instruction* (NIH Publication No. 00-4769). Washington, DC: U.S. Government Printing Office.
Website: http://www.nichd.nih.gov/publications/nrp/smallbook.htm

Palmer, C., & Kelly, M. (1992). Linguistic prosody and musical meter in song. *Journal of Memory and Language,* 31, 525-541.

Taylor, Graves, van den Broek (2000). *Reading for Meaning: Fostering Comprehension in the Middle Grades. Language and Literacy Series.* (ED435980) International Reading Association, 800 Barksdale Road, P.O. Box 8139, Newark, DE 19714-8139.

Van den Broek, P., & Kremer, K. (2000). "The mind in action: What it means to comprehend during reading." In Taylor, B., Graves, M., & Van Den Broek (Eds.). *Reading for meaning: Fostering comprehension in the middle grades.* New York, NY: Teachers College Press.

The Heinle Picture Dictionary for Children

Pictures Plus a World of Fun!

The Heinle Picture Dictionary for Children is the *only* children's dictionary that presents vocabulary within thematic readings and offers opportunities for multilevel practice of *every* word introduced to help develop English language skills.

- **1,100 words are taught contextually** through colorful illustrations and photographs, readings, and activities in eight thematic units.
- Students encounter words in context through **"Rhyme Time"** and **"Fun Facts"** readings.
- **"Playing with Words"** offers fun activities in which students increase semantic understanding and develop their language skills.

"Rhyme Time" and **"Fun Facts"** readings featured in each lesson present vocabulary in context through enjoyable readings that are sure to engage your students.

Vocabulary words appear directly next to the corresponding image to help your students make the connection between word and image.

"Playing with Words" activities give students opportunities to demonstrate their language development and apply semantic awareness.

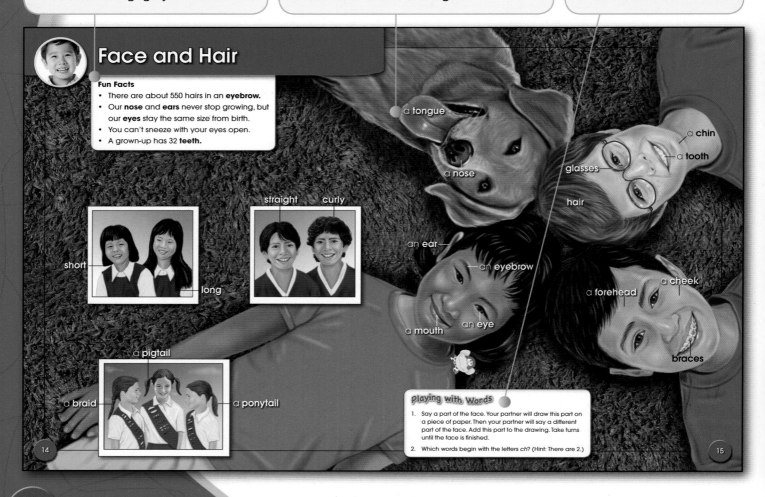

Face and Hair

Fun Facts
- There are about 550 hairs in an **eyebrow.**
- Our **nose** and **ears** never stop growing, but our **eyes** stay the same size from birth.
- You can't sneeze with your eyes open.
- A grown-up has 32 **teeth.**

a tongue
a nose
a chin
a tooth
glasses
hair
an ear
an eyebrow
a cheek
a forehead
a mouth
an eye
braces

straight   curly
short   long

a pigtail
a braid   a ponytail

playing with Words

1. Say a part of the face. Your partner will draw this part on a piece of paper. Then your partner will say a different part of the face. Add this part to the drawing. Take turns until the face is finished.
2. Which words begin with the letters *ch*? (Hint: There are 2.)

14

15

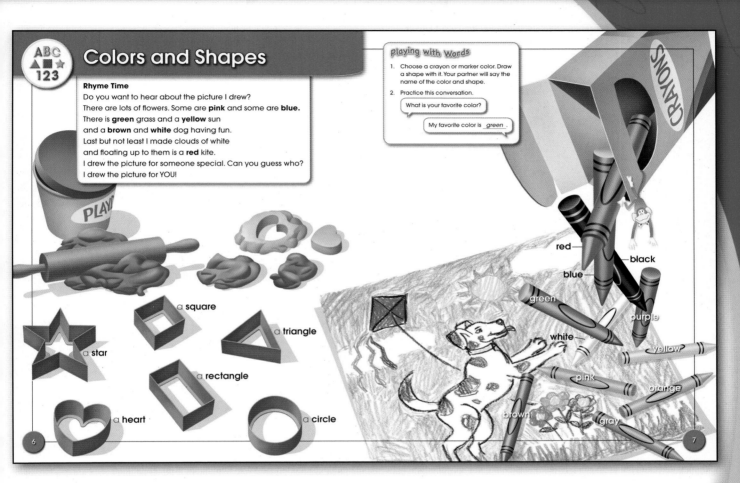

Colors and Shapes

Rhyme Time

Do you want to hear about the picture I drew?
There are lots of flowers. Some are **pink** and some are **blue**.
There is **green** grass and a **yellow** sun
and a **brown** and **white** dog having fun.
Last but not least I made clouds of white
and floating up to them is a **red** kite.
I drew the picture for someone special. Can you guess who?
I drew the picture for YOU!

Playing with Words

1. Choose a crayon or marker color. Draw a shape with it. Your partner will say the name of the color and shape.
2. Practice this conversation.

What is your favorite color?

My favorite color is green .

a square

a triangle

a star

a rectangle

a heart

a circle

red — black
blue
green
purple
white
yellow
pink
orange
brown
gray

The Heinle Picture Dictionary for Children begins with a beginning unit that features six lessons including "Letters;" "Numbers;" "Colors and Shapes;" "In, On, Over;" "Opposites;" and "Time." These lessons introduce important basic vocabulary that will jump start your students' language acquisition.

Units 2–8 explore other areas of the learner's life including their family, neighborhood, school, and the world.

Can you find the monkey?

This fun character encourages exploration as students start each lesson. They will enjoy finding the monkey every time they turn the page!

Support Materials for *The Heinle Picture Dictionary for Children*

Lesson Planner

The multilevel Lesson Planner provides three different 'mini-lessons' for each level focusing on vocabulary, phonics, and language development. The Lesson Planner is a must-have teaching tool. With three levels of instruction, it provides ample support for teachers with multilevel classrooms.

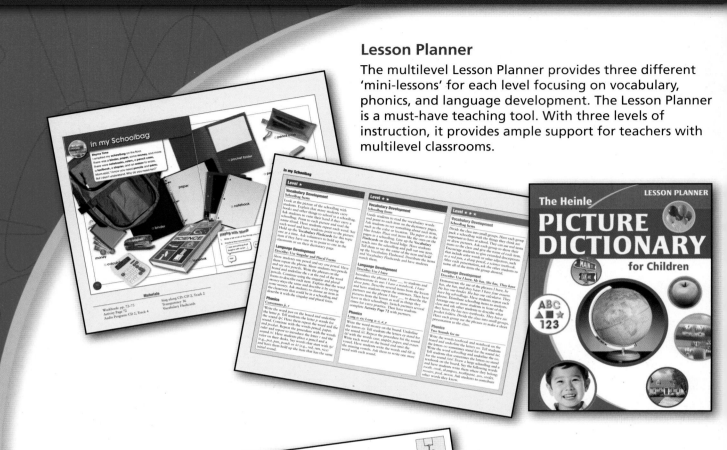

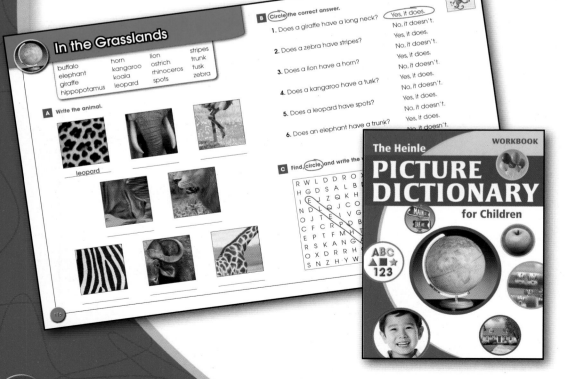

Workbook

The Workbook provides extra practice in vocabulary and language development. This colorful addition also helps students solidify new vocabulary and develop phonemic and graphemic awareness.

Interactive CD-ROM

The Interactive CD-ROM includes engaging activities such as flashcards, matching, and spelling for fun extra practice to reinforce language skills.

 *My **body**! Your **body**!*
*Everybody's **body** is so smart.*
*My **body**! Your **body**! Come*
on everybody, name the parts!
***Shoulders** roll around.*
***Arms** move up and down.*
***Elbows** bend at the joint.*
***Hands** wave. **Fingers** point!*

Sing-Along Audio CD

An entertaining and engaging Sing-Along Audio CD includes 63 original songs (one song per lesson) that recycle and reinforce the vocabulary (in bold) that students are learning in the dictionary.

Activity Bank CD-ROM

The Activity Bank CD-ROM contains ample resources to make life easier for teachers. These resources include:
- one literacy worksheet for each lesson
- activity pages for use with minilessons in the Lesson Planner
- vocabulary flashcards for each lesson
- reproducible activity masters including graphic organizers and games
- an alphabetical word list for each lesson
- each reading from the dictionary in a customizable format
- song lyrics from the Sing-Along Audio CD

Letters

Rhyme Time

Where would we be
without **A, B,** and **C?**
We'd have no *ant, bird,* or *cat.*
Can you imagine that?
And without **D, E,** and **F,** we'd have to say good-bye
to *dog* and to *elephant*, and even to *fly.*
We need the letters from A to **Z.**
Each one is important. Don't you agree?

apple
ant

bird
boy
Bb

cat
Cc
cake

dinosaur
Dd
dog

elephant
Ee
egg

fly
Ff
frog

gift
Gg
girl

horse
house
Hh

ice cream
Ii
igloo

jump rope
Jj
jellyfish

kite
Kk
kangaroo

lion
Ll
leaf

man

Mm

mouse

owl

Nn

necklace

nut

Oo

orange

pig

Pp

pencil

quilt

Qq

queen

rainbow

Rr

rabbit

seal

Ss

strawberry

tree

Tt

train

umbrella

Uu

unicorn

volcano

Vv

violin

woman

Ww

wagon

X-ray

Xx

xylophone

zebra

Yy

yo-yo

yarn

Zz

zipper

playing with Words

1. Trace a letter on your partner's hand. Your partner will guess the letter. Take turns.

2. Say a letter to your partner. Your partner will think of a word that starts with the letter. Take turns.

Numbers

Rhyme Time

My mother gave me **one** ball. The ball is blue.
My dad gave me another. Then I had **two.**
Grandma gave a red one to me.
One plus one plus one is **three.**
My friend gave me one, so now I have **four.**
I really don't need any more!

1   one

2   two

3   three

4   four

5   five

6   six

7   seven

8   eight

9   nine

10   ten

11   eleven

12   twelve

13   thirteen

14   fourteen

15   fifteen

16   sixteen

17   seventeen

18   eighteen

19   nineteen

20   twenty

first

second

third

fourth

fifth

plus   equals

$1 + 1 = 2$

minus

$2 - 1 = 1$

Playing with Words

1. How many of these are in your class: Teachers? Students? Girls? Boys?

2. Practice this conversation.

How old are you?   I'm _7_ years old.

Rhyme Time

Do you want to hear about the picture I drew?

There are lots of flowers. Some are **pink** and some are **blue.**

There is **green** grass and a **yellow** sun

and a **brown** and **white** dog having fun.

Last but not least I made clouds of white

and floating up to them is a **red** kite.

I drew the picture for someone special. Can you guess who?

I drew the picture for YOU!

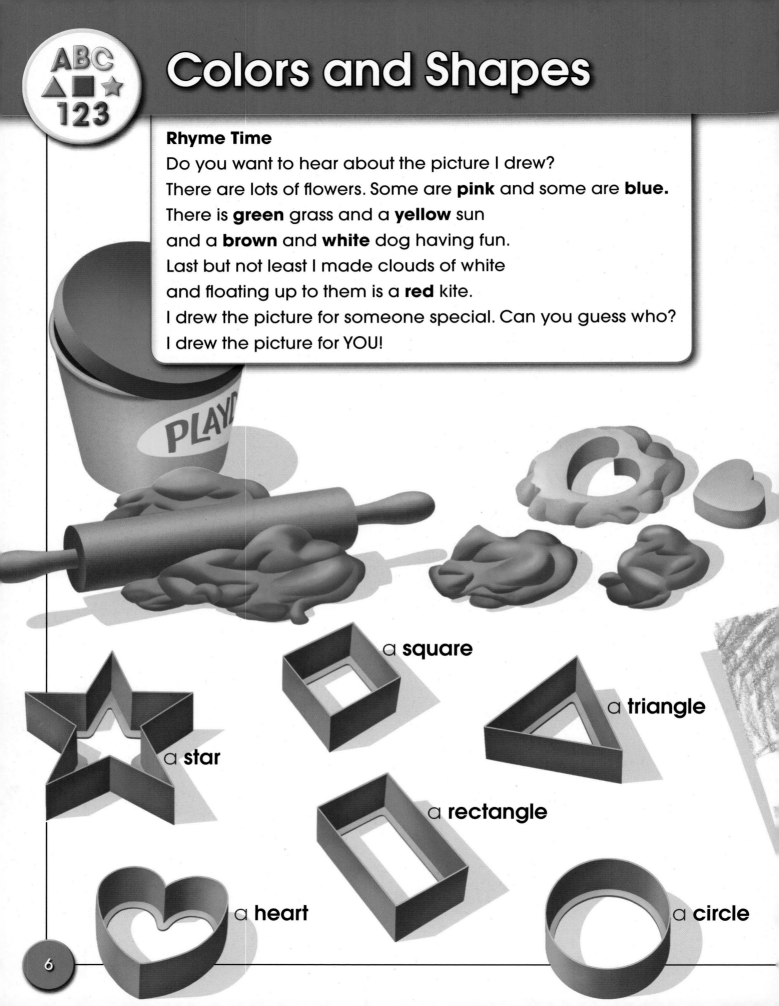

a **square**

a **triangle**

a **star**

a **rectangle**

a **heart**

a **circle**

PLAYD

6

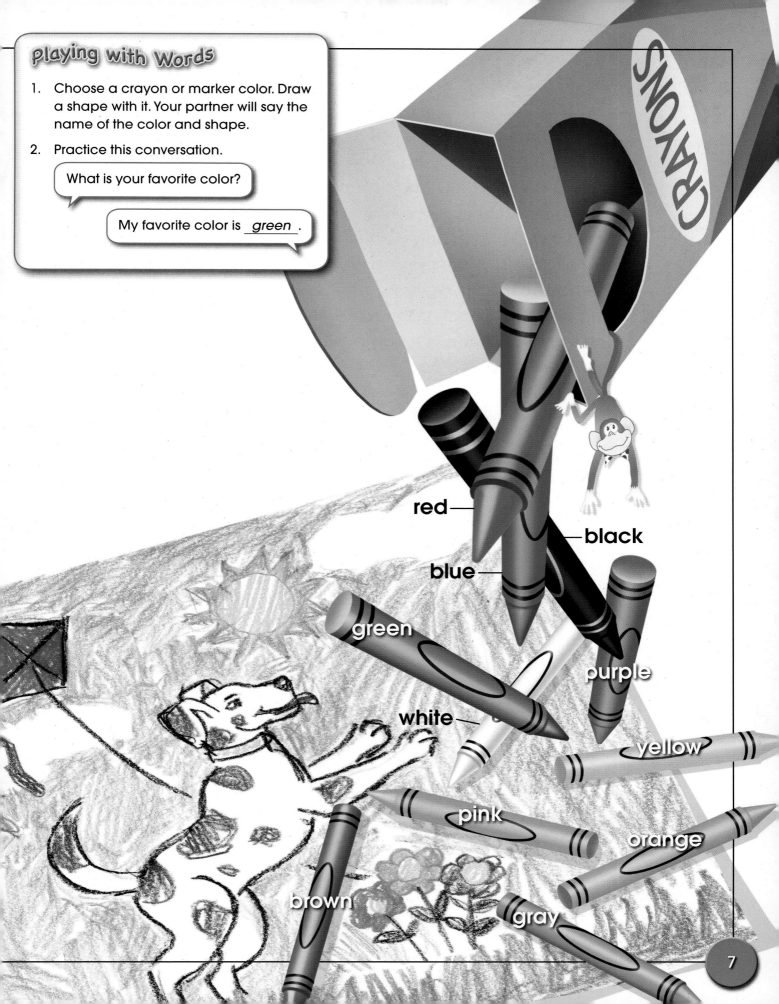

playing with Words

1. Choose a crayon or marker color. Draw a shape with it. Your partner will say the name of the color and shape.

2. Practice this conversation.

What is your favorite color?

My favorite color is _green_ .

red—

—black

blue—

green

purple

white—

yellow

pink

orange

brown

gray

In, On, Over

Rhyme Time

My friend Henri is looking for me.

Do you see him there? He's **above** Lee.

I like to hide. My name is Aki.

I'm **in** the red box. (Don't tell Henri!)

Lots of other kids are playing too.

The boy **on** the bridge is my friend Stu.

And do you see that girl **in front of** him?

She's my best friend. Her name is Kim.

And there is Debbie going **down** the slide.

We're all having fun while playing outside.

The dog is running **around** the tree.

Jen is jumping **over** Chris.

Jen

Chris — Chris is **under** Jen.

Safia is **across from** Elisa.

Olga

Olga is **next to** Safia.

Safia

Paco is **on the right of** Elisa.

Elisa

Paco

Debbie

Elisa is **on the left of** Paco.

Debbie is going **down** the slide.

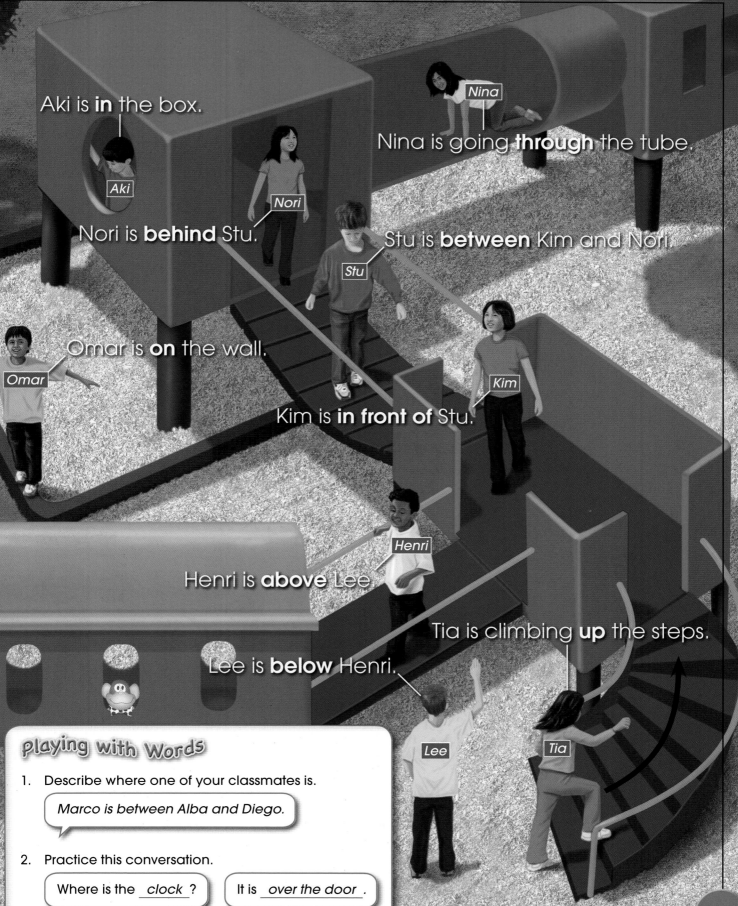

Aki is **in** the box.

Nina is going **through** the tube.

Nori is **behind** Stu.

Stu is **between** Kim and Nori.

Omar is **on** the wall.

Kim is **in front of** Stu.

Henri is **above** Lee

Tia is climbing **up** the steps.

Lee is **below** Henri.

Playing with Words

1. Describe where one of your classmates is.

   Marco is between Alba and Diego.

2. Practice this conversation.

   Where is the _clock_ ?   It is _over the door_ .

9

Opposites

Rhyme Time

Tell me, tell me: What is **small?**
A bug, a coin, a grape, a mouse.
Tell me, tell me: What is **big?**
An elephant, a bus, a house.

Tell me, tell me: What is **loud?**
Crying babies, banging drums.
Tell me, tell me: What is **quiet?**
Little babies sucking their thumbs.

Tell me, tell me: What is **clean?**
New shoes and floors swept with a broom.
Tell me, tell me: What is **dirty?**
My shirt, my hands, my face, my room!

new

old

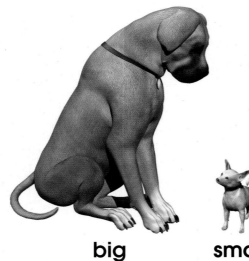

big   small

quiet   loud

dirty

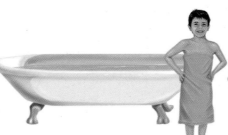

clean

open   **closed**   **young**   **old**

slow   **fast**

long

short

short   **tall**

Time

Rhyme Time
Thirty **days** has **September,**
April, June, and **November.**
All the rest have thirty-one,
except **February.**
February has twenty-eight days most of the time.
But one year in four it has twenty-nine.

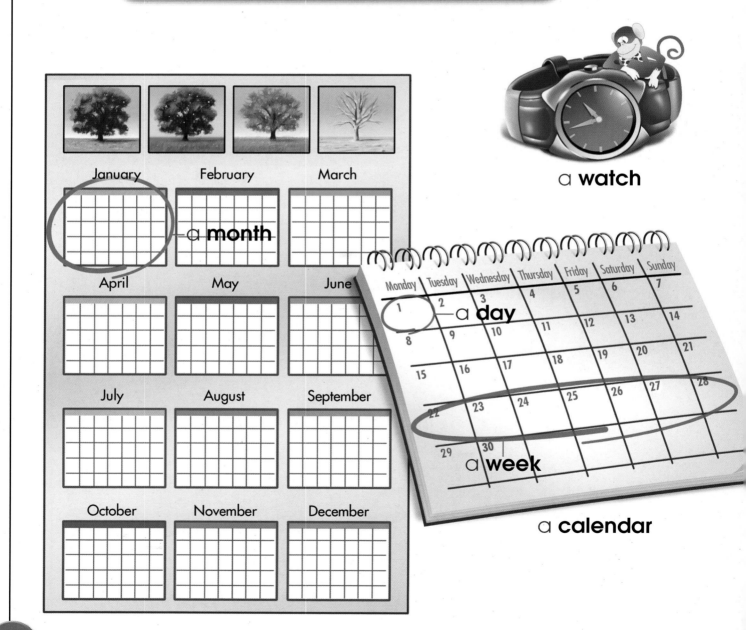

January   February   March

a **month**

April   May   June

July   August   September

October   November   December

a **watch**

Monday	Tuesday	Wednesday	Thursday	Friday	Saturday	Sunday
1	2	3	4	5	6	7
8	9	10	11	12	13	14
15	16	17	18	19	20	21
22	23	24	25	26	27	28
29	30					

a **day**

a **week**

a **calendar**

a **clock**

morning

1:00 / one o'clock

1:15 / one fifteen

afternoon

1:30 / one thirty

1:45 / one forty-five

evening

night

playing with Words

1. Look at the words. Make 2 lists:
   - days I go to school
   - days I stay home

2. Practice this conversation.

My birthday is in _November_ . When is yours?

Mine is in _June_ .

13

Face and Hair

Fun Facts

- There are about 550 hairs in an **eyebrow.**
- Our **nose** and **ears** never stop growing, but our **eyes** stay the same size from birth.
- You can't sneeze with your eyes open.
- A grown-up has 32 **teeth.**

straight   curly

short

long

a **pigtail**

a **braid**   a **ponytail**

a tongue

a chin

a tooth

glasses

a nose

hair

an ear

an eyebrow

a cheek

a forehead

an eye

a mouth

braces

Playing with Words

1. Say a part of the face. Your partner will draw this part on a piece of paper. Then your partner will say a different part of the face. Add this part to the drawing. Take turns until the face is finished.

2. Which words begin with the letters *ch*? (Hint: There are 2.)

Body

Fun Facts

- More than half of your **body** is made of water.
- Half the bones in your body are in your **hands** and feet.
- You have about 100,000 hairs on your **head.**
- The nails on your **fingers** grow faster than the nails on your **toes.**
- The length from your **wrist** to your **elbow** is the same as the length of your **foot.**

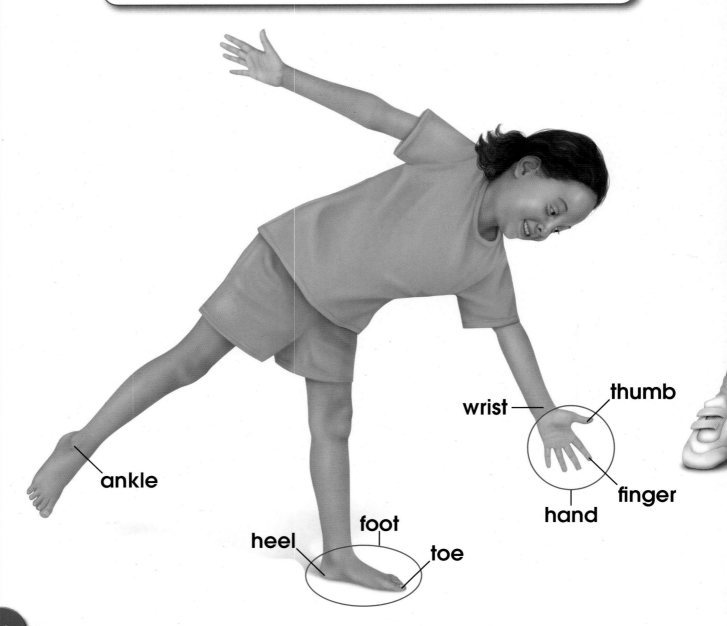

ankle

wrist — thumb

hand — finger

heel — foot — toe

head

arm

chest

stomach

back

shoulder

neck

knee

leg

elbow

Playing with Words

1. Touch a part of your body. Your partner will say the name. Take turns.

That's your _nose_ !

2. Which words have 4 letters? (Hint: There are 7.)

17

Clothes 1

Rhyme Time
Mom took me shopping for new **clothes.**
Can you guess the things that we chose?
We bought some **jeans,** a **jacket,** a **skirt,**
a pair of **sneakers** and three **T-shirts.**
We also bought a **necklace,** a **bracelet,** and a **ring.**
Dad said, "The store must be empty. You bought everything!"

a **sweatshirt**

jeans

a **sneaker** —

a **blouse** —

a **jacket**

a **skirt**

tights —

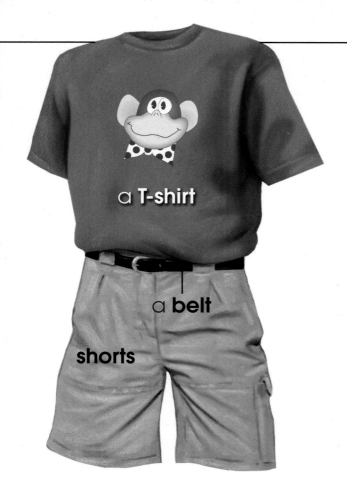

a T-shirt

a belt

shorts

an **undershirt**

underpants

underwear

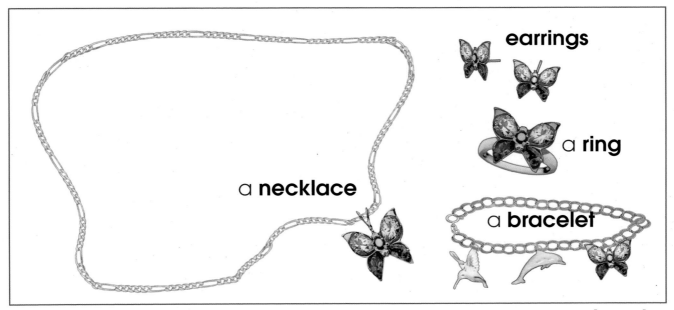

earrings

a **ring**

a **necklace**

a **bracelet**

jewelry

playing with Words

1. Finish the sentence.
   Today, I am wearing _ *a sweatshirt* _.

2. Find the words that have "shirt" in them. (Hint: There are 3.)

Clothes 2

Rhyme Time

I start each day with clean **clothes**

but soon I'm a mess from my head to my toes.

Yesterday I played sports.

I fell down and ripped my shorts.

Then I played in the dirt

and got mud on my new **shirt.**

Then somehow I got rocks

inside my **shoes** and in my **socks.**

I know it's really hard to believe,

but I even ripped off my sweatshirt **sleeve!**

a **hat**

 a **baseball cap**

a **coat**

a **scarf**

a **sweater**

a **glove**

pants

a **shoe**

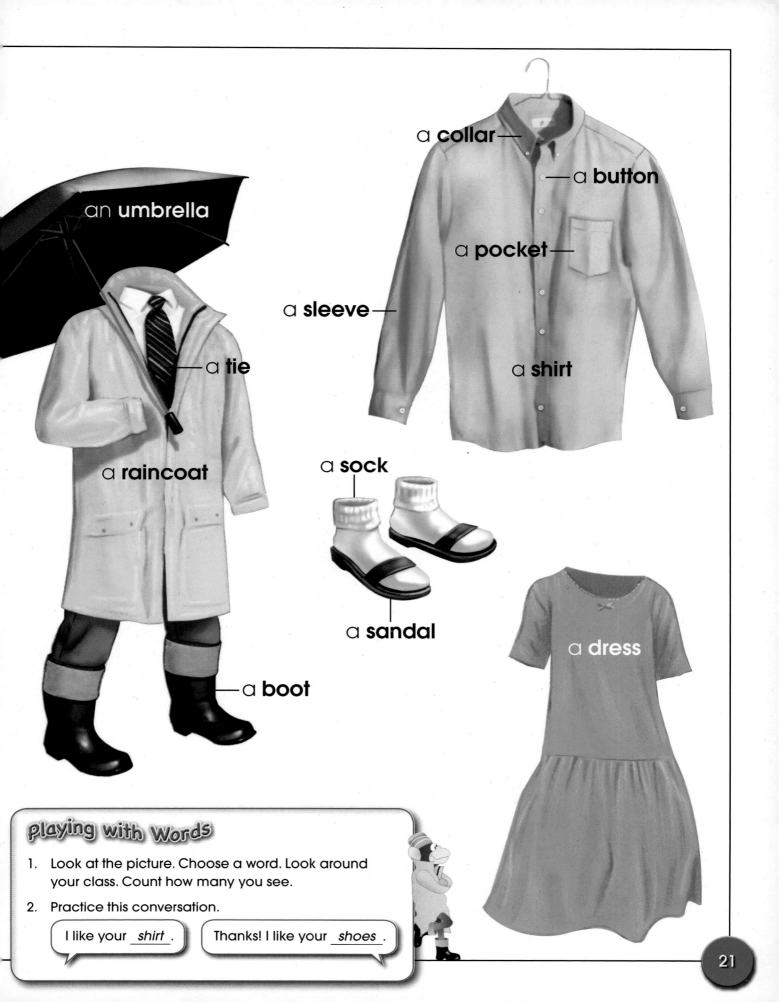

an **umbrella**

a **collar**

a **button**

a **pocket**

a **sleeve**

a **shirt**

a **tie**

a **raincoat**

a **sock**

a **sandal**

a **dress**

a **boot**

My Family

Rhyme Time

My teacher asked us to make a family tree.
First I started with a picture of **me.**
I added pictures of my **sister** and **brother**
and above us I added my **father** and **mother.**
Then I thought of some more people to add,
like my **aunt** and my **uncle** (the brother of my **dad**).
I added my **cousins** and then four others:
I'd never forget my **grandfathers** and **grandmothers!**

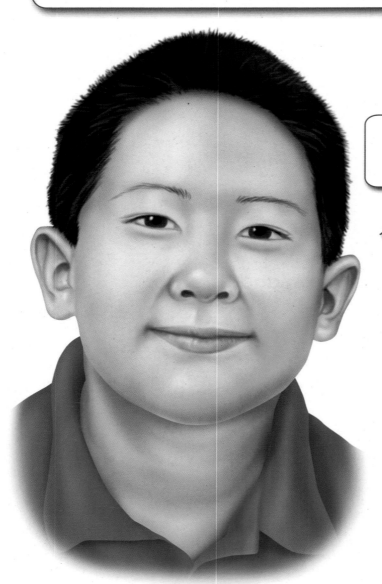

Hi, I'm Akio.
This is my family.

grandparents

grandmother / grandma **grandfather / grandpa**

grandparents

grandmother / grandma **grandfather / grandpa**

parents

uncle

mother / mom **father / dad**

aunt **uncle**

sister **me** **brother**

cousin **cousin**

Playing with Words

1. Cover one of the words. Ask your partner who the person is. Take turns.

   Who is this?   That's Akio *'s sister* .

2. Tell your partner the name of someone in your family. Take turns.

   My _*mother*_'s name is _*Alba*_ .

Feelings

Rhyme Time

I've had so many **feelings** in just one day.

My friend came to my house to play.

We drew pictures of animals. She made a giraffe.

It was so **silly.** I had to **laugh.**

She broke my toy. That made me **mad.**

But when she went home I still felt **sad.**

happy

smile

sad

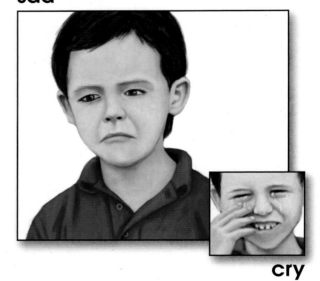

cry

mad

yell

scared

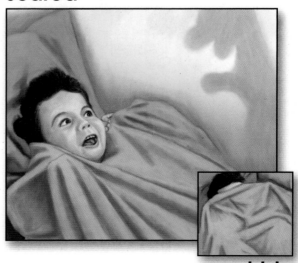

hide

silly

laugh

hungry

eat

thirsty

drink

tired

yawn

Playing with Words

1. Pretend to feel one of these feelings. Your partner will guess the feeling. Take turns.

2. Practice this conversation.

How do you feel right now?   I feel _tired_ .

My Day

Rhyme Time

Every morning I want to **sleep** for one more hour.

But instead I **get up, make my bed,** and **take a shower.**

I rush so I won't be late for school,

where I learn, have fun, and follow rules.

After school, there are many things to do.

I **play** with friends, **eat** dinner, and **do homework** too.

I always want to stay up late but instead

my mother says, "You've had a busy **day.** Now **go** to bed!"

I **get up.**

I **make my bed.**

I **take a shower.**

I **get dressed.**

I **brush my teeth.**

I **eat** breakfast.

I **go** to school.

I **eat** lunch.

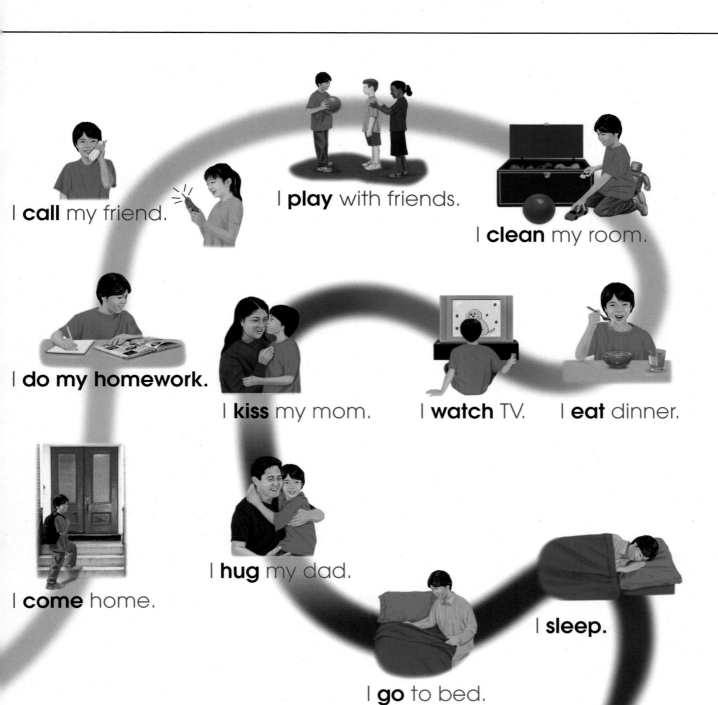

I **call** my friend.

I **play** with friends.

I **clean** my room.

I **do my homework.**

I **kiss** my mom.

I **watch** TV.

I **eat** dinner.

I **come** home.

I **hug** my dad.

I **go** to bed.

I **sleep.**

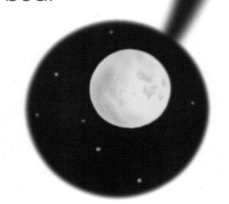

playing with Words

1. What are your 3 favorite things to do each day? What are the 3 things you least like to do? Tell your partner.

2. Practice this conversation.

   What do you do at __1:00__ each day?

   I __eat lunch__ .

In the Kitchen

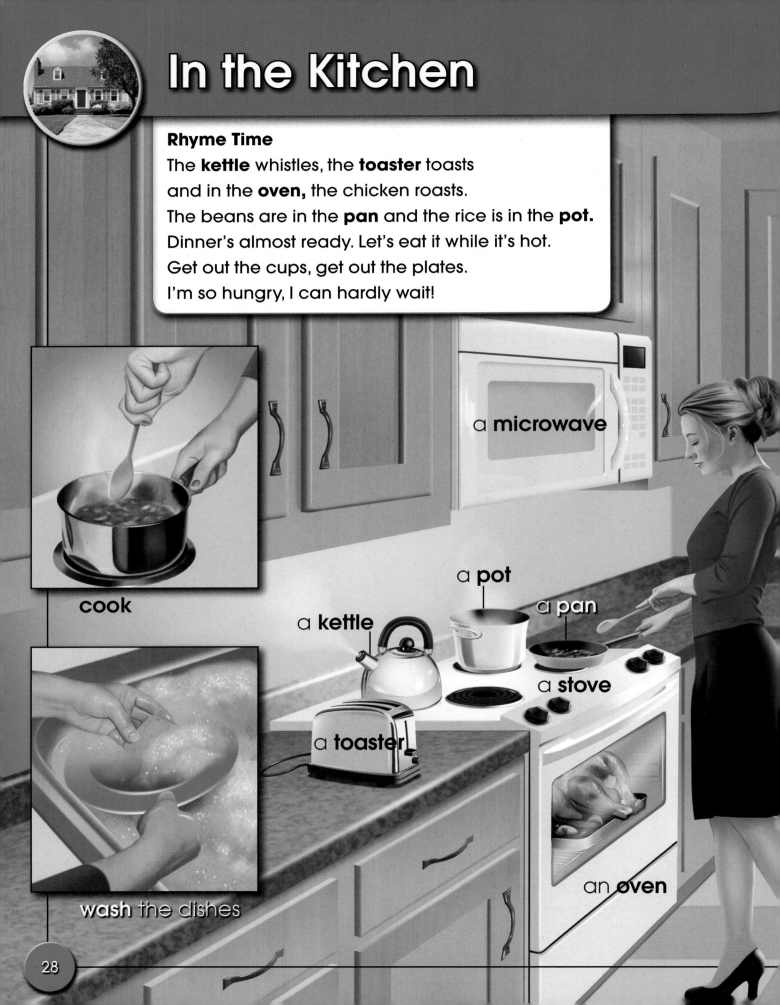

Rhyme Time

The **kettle** whistles, the **toaster** toasts
and in the **oven,** the chicken roasts.
The beans are in the **pan** and the rice is in the **pot.**
Dinner's almost ready. Let's eat it while it's hot.
Get out the cups, get out the plates.
I'm so hungry, I can hardly wait!

cook

wash the dishes

a **microwave**

a **pot**

a **kettle**

a **pan**

a **stove**

a **toaster**

an **oven**

Playing with Words

1. Pretend to use one of the things in the kitchen. Your partner will guess what you are using. Take turns.

2. Which words start with the letter *p*? (Hint: There are 2.)

a refrigerator

a counter

a drawer

a cabinet

29

In the Living Room

Rhyme Time

When the day is over and dinner is done,
in the **living room** we relax and have fun.
Sometimes we watch **TV,** just us four,
or play around on the **floor.**
With mom on the **couch** and me by her knee,
I love it when she reads to me.
When it gets dark, we turn on the **light**
to keep the room cozy and bright.

a **plant**

a **couch**

a **lamp**

a **CD player**

a **telephone**

earphones

a **coffee table**

a **rug**

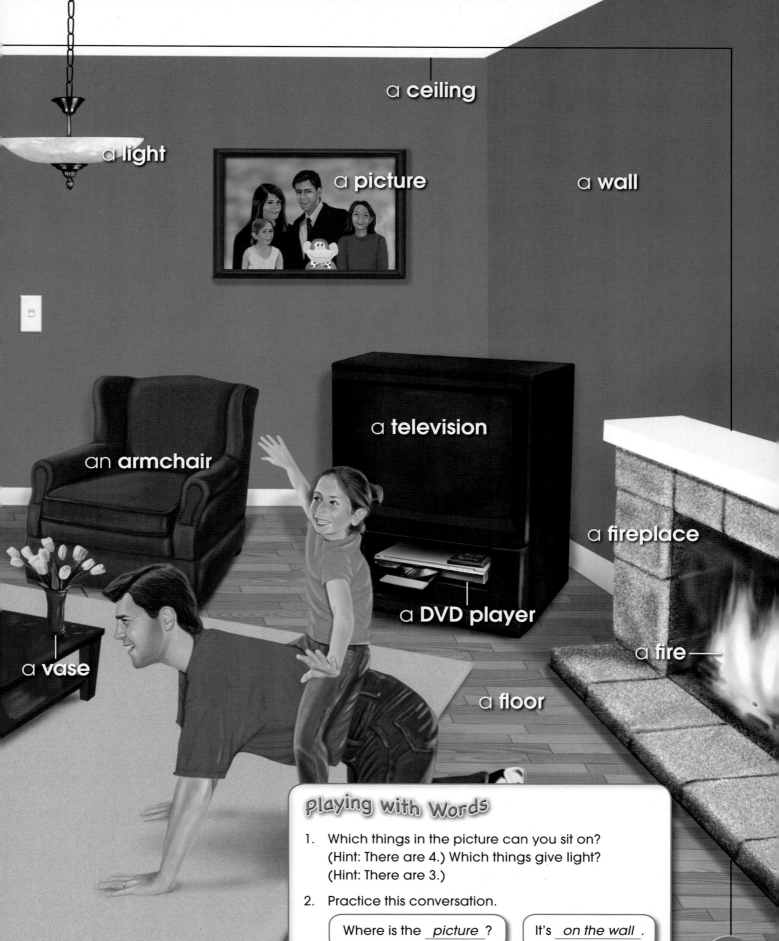

a ceiling

a light

a picture

a wall

a television

an armchair

a fireplace

a DVD player

a fire

a vase

a floor

Playing with Words

1. Which things in the picture can you sit on?
   (Hint: There are 4.) Which things give light?
   (Hint: There are 3.)

2. Practice this conversation.

   Where is the _picture_ ?   It's _on the wall_ .

In the Bedroom

Rhyme Time

My mother said, "Your **bedroom** is a mess.

Will you clean it up?" I said, "Yes."

I picked up my clothes and my dirty socks.

I put away my toys in my big **toy box.**

I changed the **sheets** on my **bed.**

Then Mom came back and to me she said,

"It's so neat and clean! Whose room is this?"

Then she laughed and laughed and gave me a kiss.

a **dresser**

a **bed**

a **pillow**

an **alarm clock**

a **lamp**

stuffed animals

a **blanket**

a **sheet**

a **comforter**

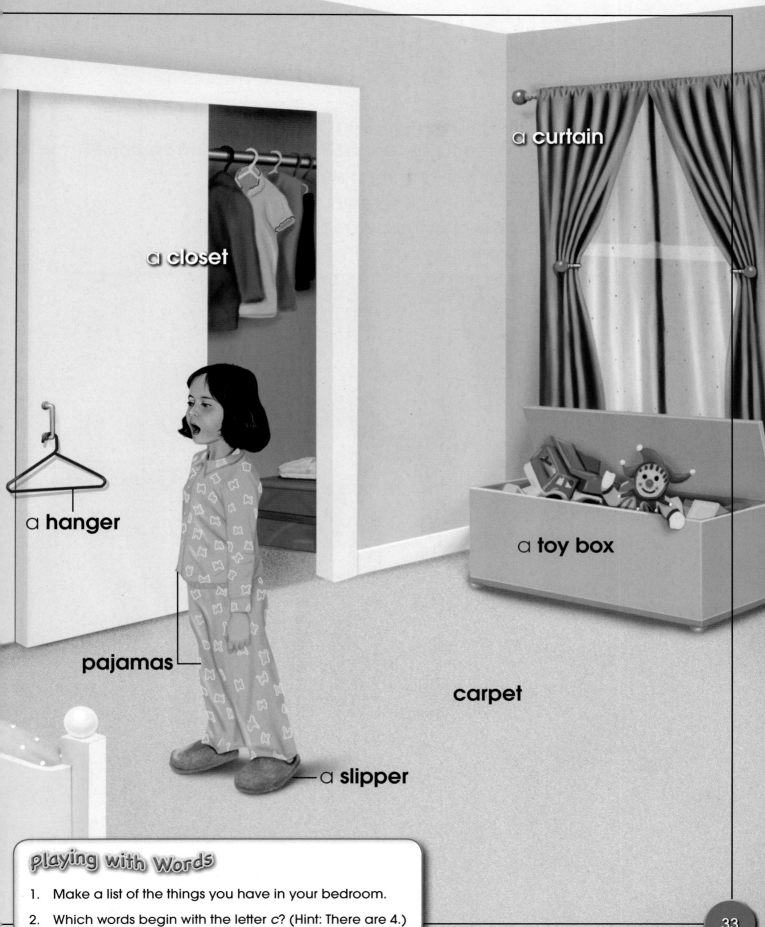

a curtain

a closet

a hanger

pajamas

a slipper

a toy box

carpet

Playing with Words

1. Make a list of the things you have in your bedroom.

2. Which words begin with the letter *c*? (Hint: There are 4.)

In the Bathroom

Rhyme Time

The **bathroom** is the busiest room in our home.

Mom says, "Who took the **brush?**" Dad says, "I need the **comb!**"

My sister says, "I need to take a **shower.**"

I say, "Oh no! You'll take an hour!"

I can't find the **toothpaste.** We're out of **shampoo.**

This place is a little like a zoo!

a **towel**

a **washcloth**

a **shower**

shampoo

soap

a **bathtub**

a **bath mat**

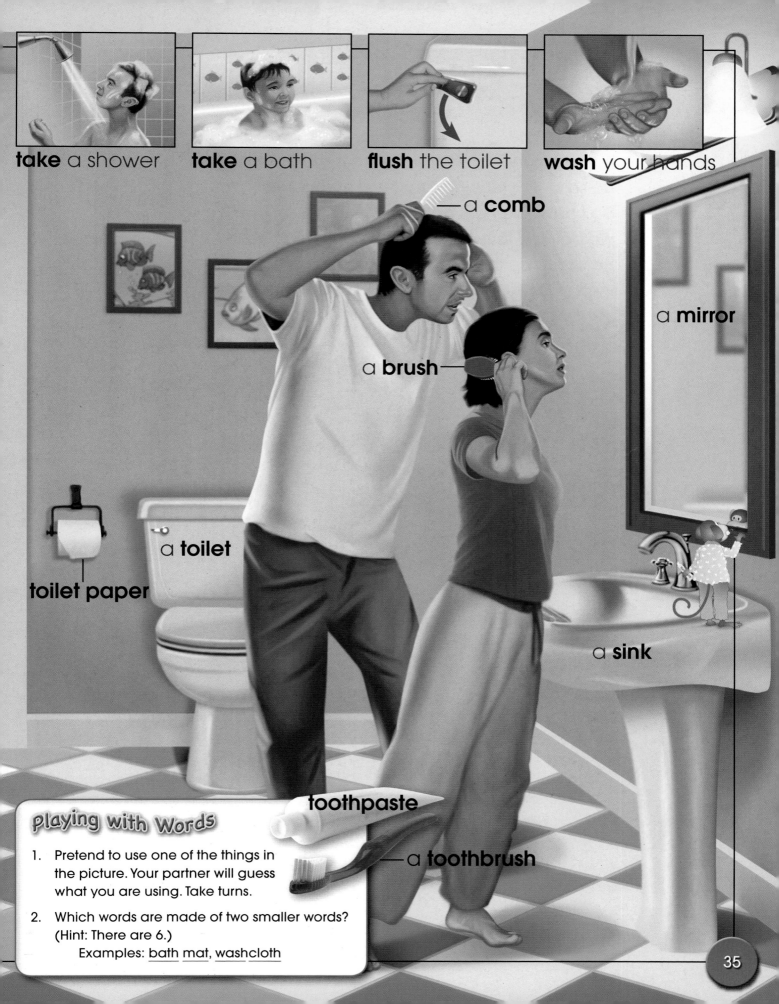

take a shower

take a bath

flush the toilet

wash your hands

a comb

a mirror

a brush

a toilet

toilet paper

a sink

toothpaste

a toothbrush

Playing with Words

1. Pretend to use one of the things in the picture. Your partner will guess what you are using. Take turns.

2. Which words are made of two smaller words? (Hint: There are 6.)
   Examples: <u>bath</u> <u>mat</u>, <u>washcloth</u>

Outside the House

Rhyme Time

A **mail carrier** came through our **gate**.

He said, "I'm looking for **house** number 48.

Do I have the right **address?"**

We pointed to the number and told him, "Yes."

He came up the **steps** and to the **door**

then realized the mail was for house number 44!

a **chimney**

a **roof**

a **window**

an **address**

Anna Stewart
44 Bow Street
Concord, CA 93021

48

a **door**

a **porch**

a **mail carrier**

a **gate**

a **step**

a **wagon**

a tree house

a house

a neighbor

a helmet

a tricycle

a fence

a driveway

a yard

playing with Words

1. Say one of the parts of a house. Your partner will draw it. Take turns.

2. Find the word that begins with the letter *y*. Find the words that end with the letter *y*. (Hint: There are 2.)

In the Garage

a **saw**

a **drill**

a **hammer**

a **screwdriver**

a **nail**

a **tape measure**

a **battery**

a **wrench**

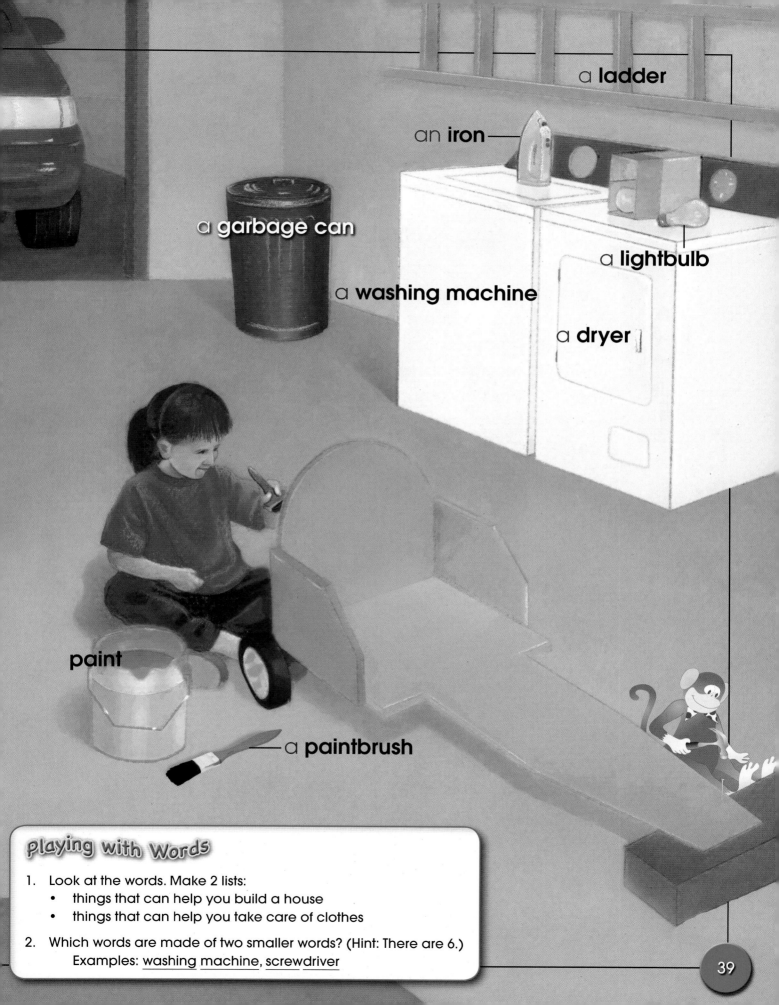

a ladder

an **iron**

a **garbage can**

a **washing machine**

a **lightbulb**

a **dryer**

paint

a **paintbrush**

Playing with Words

1. Look at the words. Make 2 lists:
   - things that can help you build a house
   - things that can help you take care of clothes

2. Which words are made of two smaller words? (Hint: There are 6.)
   Examples: <u>washing</u> <u>machine</u>, <u>screw</u><u>driver</u>

On the Move

Rhyme Time

Last night I dreamed I took a trip.

I stepped onto a big, old **ship.**

Later I got on a **train.**

I think it was on the way to Spain.

Then I bought a big, red **car**

and drove it really, really far.

Finally I went up in a **hot air balloon**

and floated all the month of June.

I thought I was far from home but instead,

when I opened my eyes, I was back in bed!

a **ship**

a **sailboat**

a **ferry**

a **truck**

a **car**

a **van**

a **road**

a **motorcycle**

a **bridge**

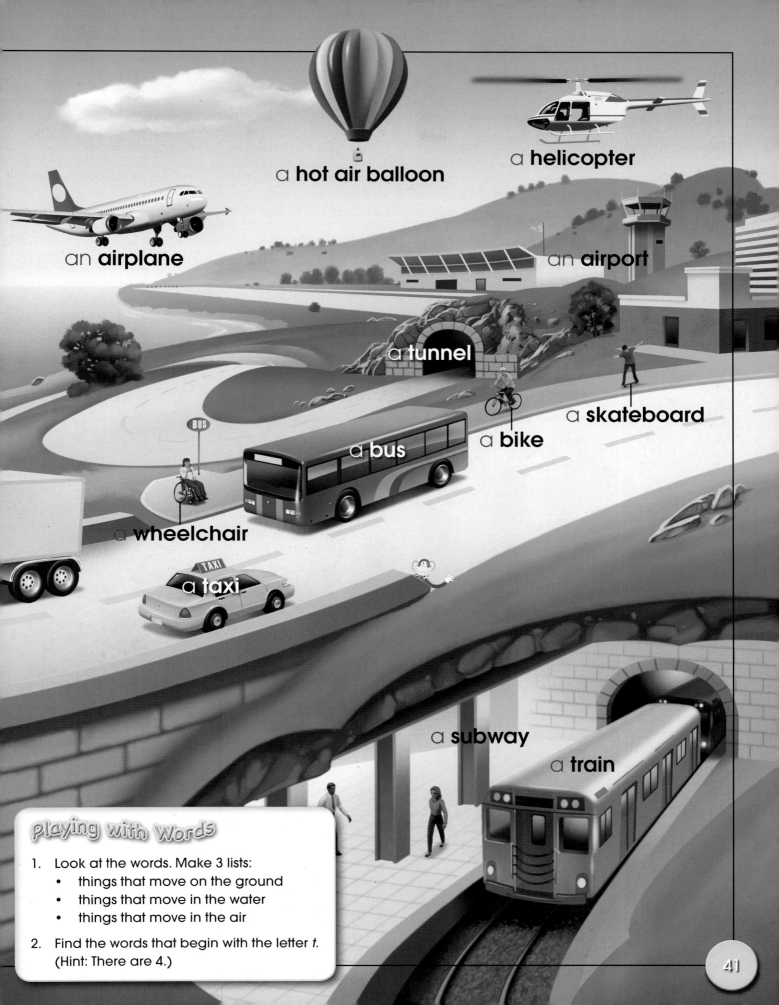

a hot air balloon

a helicopter

an airplane

an airport

a tunnel

a skateboard

a bus

a bike

a wheelchair

a taxi

a subway

a train

playing with Words

1. Look at the words. Make 3 lists:
   - things that move on the ground
   - things that move in the water
   - things that move in the air

2. Find the words that begin with the letter *t*.
   (Hint: There are 4.)

41

Around Town

MAIN ST
OAK AVE

Rhyme Time

Ted. Ted. Where is Ted?

He's at the **bakery** getting bread.

Frank. Frank. Where is Frank?

He's getting money at the **bank.**

Pat. Pat. Where is Pat?

She's washing clothes at the **laundromat.**

Raul. Raul. Where is Raul?

He's learning numbers and letters at **school.**

Pete. Pete. Where is Pete?

He's waiting for you on the **street.**

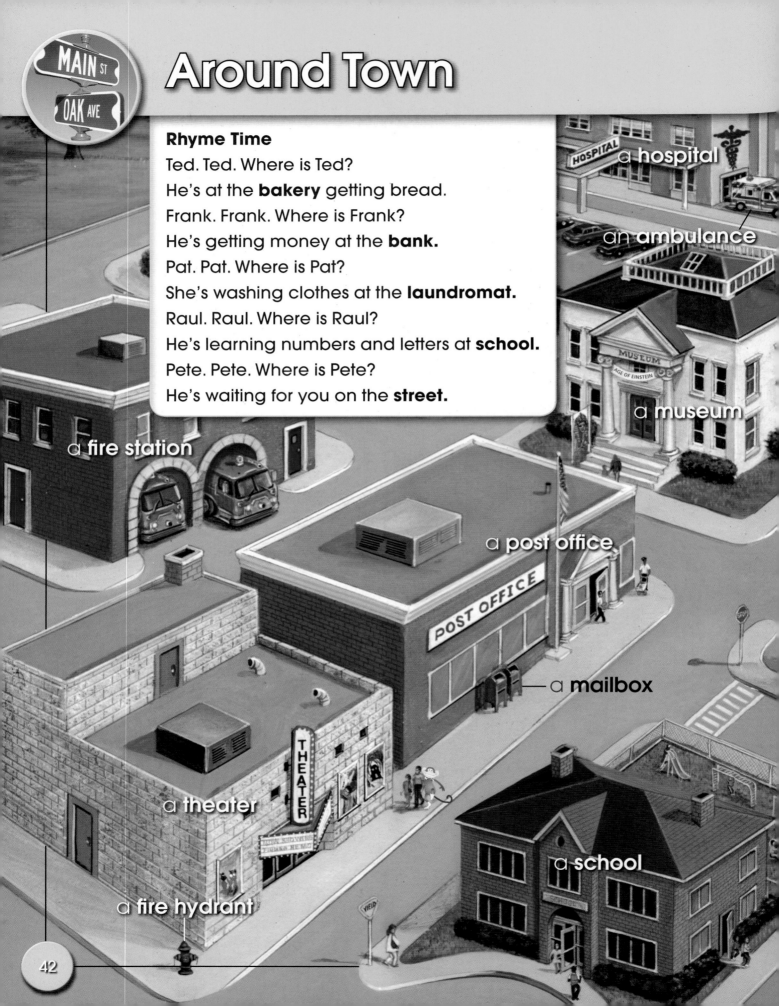

a **hospital**

an **ambulance**

a **museum**

a **fire station**

a **post office**

a **mailbox**

a **theater**

a **school**

a **fire hydrant**

42

a factory

a train station

a supermarket

SUPERMARKET

an apartment building

a bank

$ BANK $

BANK

FOR RENT

a florist

CITY FLORIST

a bus stop

a crosswalk

Laundroma

a laundromat

a bakery

BAKERY

GAS

a gas station

ICE

a street

Playing with Words

1. Look at the picture. Choose one of the places. Say something you can get, see, or do in this place. Tell your partner. Take turns.

2. Which words end with the letter y? (Hint: There are 2.)

43

In the Park

Rhyme Time

There is a nice **park** in my neighborhood.
It has a nice **path,** and a **playground** that's good.
There's a **seesaw,** a **slide,** and a few **swings.**
And I haven't even told you everything.
There's also a **sandbox** to play in and **monkey bars**
to hang from.
I think I'll go there today. Do you want to come?

a **zoo**

a **trash can**

a **bench**

a **path**

a **statue**

a **sandbox**

a **kite**

a **hill**

a **picnic**

a **seesaw**

a **slide**

a **swing**

the **monkey bars**

a **ball**

a **jump rope**

a **playground**

45

Run, Jump, Throw

Rhyme Time

Let's **swing** on the swing! Let's **slide** down the slide!

There's so much to do, I just can't decide.

Let's **throw** and **catch** and **kick** the ball!

"Slow down," says the teacher, "before you **fall**!"

push

ride

pull

slide

hop

catch

swing

kick

climb

chase

run

throw

fall

jump

Playing with Words

1. Look at the words. Pretend to do one of these things. Your partner will guess what you are doing. Take turns.

2. Which word begins with the letters *ch*? Which word ends with the letters *ch*?

MAIN ST
OAK AVE

Rhyme Time

Where can I get some **books** for free?

    You can borrow them from the **library.**

Is borrowing books very hard?

    Not at all. Just get a **library card.**

Do you want to come to the library with me?

    Sure. I need to **return** a **DVD.**

a **dictionary**

a **bookshelf**

Sweet Home

Happy Stories

check out

a **videotape**

The Westdale Times

a **newspaper**

CHECKOUT

a **computer**

a **librarian**

a **checkout desk**

a **library card**

Westdale Public Library

Name

Lily Ma

Expires October 12 2011

return

an **atlas**

a **magazine**

a **book**

Once Upon a Time

Funny Movie

a **DVD**

Playing with Words

1. Look at the words. Make 2 lists:
   • things you can check out from the library
   • things you can look at or use only at the library

2. Find a word that begins with each letter: *a*, *b*, *c*, and *d*.

Pets at the Vet

Fun Facts

- A **cat** has 230 **bones** in its body. A person has 206 bones.
- An average mother cat has more than 50 **kittens** in her life.
- **Dogs** can see the colors blue, yellow, and gray. They can't see red and green.
- There are more than 9,000 kinds of **birds.**
- 94% of **pet** owners say their pets make them smile more than once a day.

a turtle

a mouse

a cage

fur

a cat —

— a kitten

a bird

a puppy

a veterinarian

a leash

a collar

a dog

a paw

a tail

a bone

a fishbowl

a fish

51

At the Mall

Rhyme Time

Mom said, "Let's go to the **mall** today."

I like the mall, so I said, "OK."

We passed the **bookstore,** the **food court,** and the **toy store.**

What was my mother looking for?

We took the **escalator** up. We took the **elevator** down.

We walked right, then left. We walked around and around.

She stopped at the **pet shop** and said, "I was looking for that."

Then she took me inside and bought me a cat!

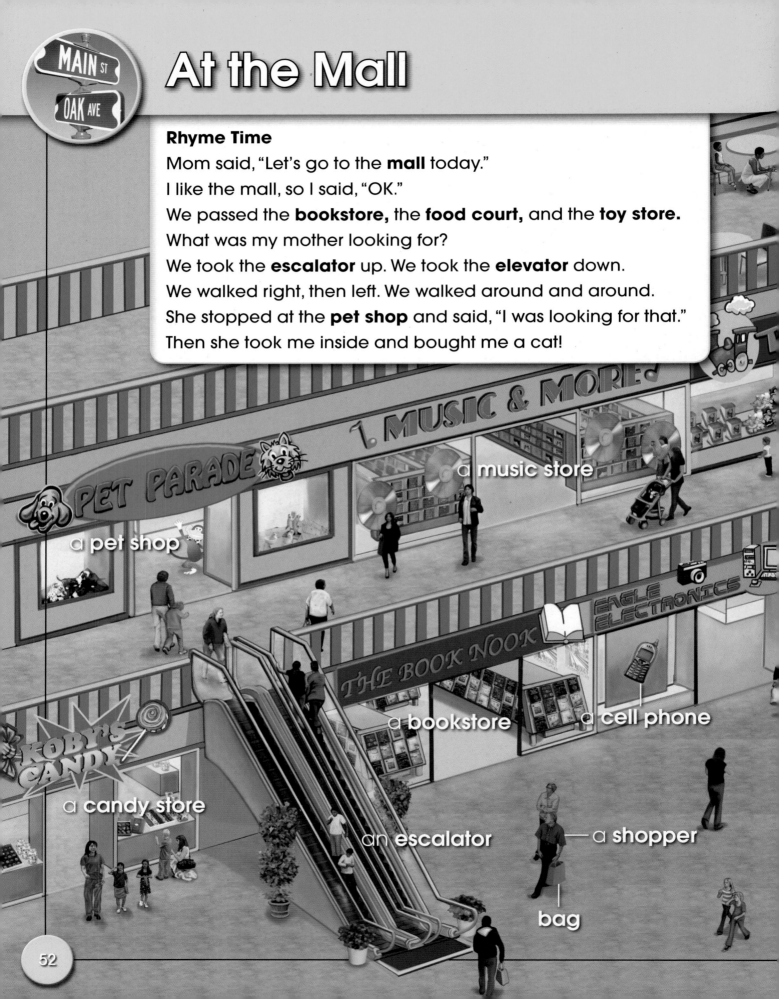

PET PARADE

1. MUSIC & MORE

a **music store**

a **pet shop**

THE BOOK NOOK

EAGLE ELECTRONICS

a **bookstore**

a **cell phone**

KOBY'S CANDY

a **candy store**

an **escalator**

a **shopper**

bag

a food court

an elevator

a toy store

a movie theater

a shoe store

a clothing store

an ATM

a restroom

Playing with Words

1. Imagine you are in this mall. What places do you want to go to? Why? Talk with a partner.

2. Practice this conversation.

   Where should we go?　　Let's go to the _food court_ .

53

At the Restaurant

Rhyme Time

Dad gives me a **menu** and asks, "What will you eat?

Would you like some vegetables and maybe some meat?"

I say, "These foods are strange. They're all new."

Dad says, "I will order something special for you."

The **waiter** takes the order and then **serves** the food.

I know I won't like it. I'm in a bad mood.

I pick up my **fork** and try the food on my **plate.**

I can't believe it. It's really great!

a chair

a table

a waiter

a tablecloth

serve

pour

stir

pass

1. Tell what you need to use to eat each of these foods: soup, chicken, milk, cereal.

2. Look at the picture. Choose a word. Say the first letter of the word. Your partner will guess the word.

This word starts with _g_ .

Is it _glass_ ?

Yes !

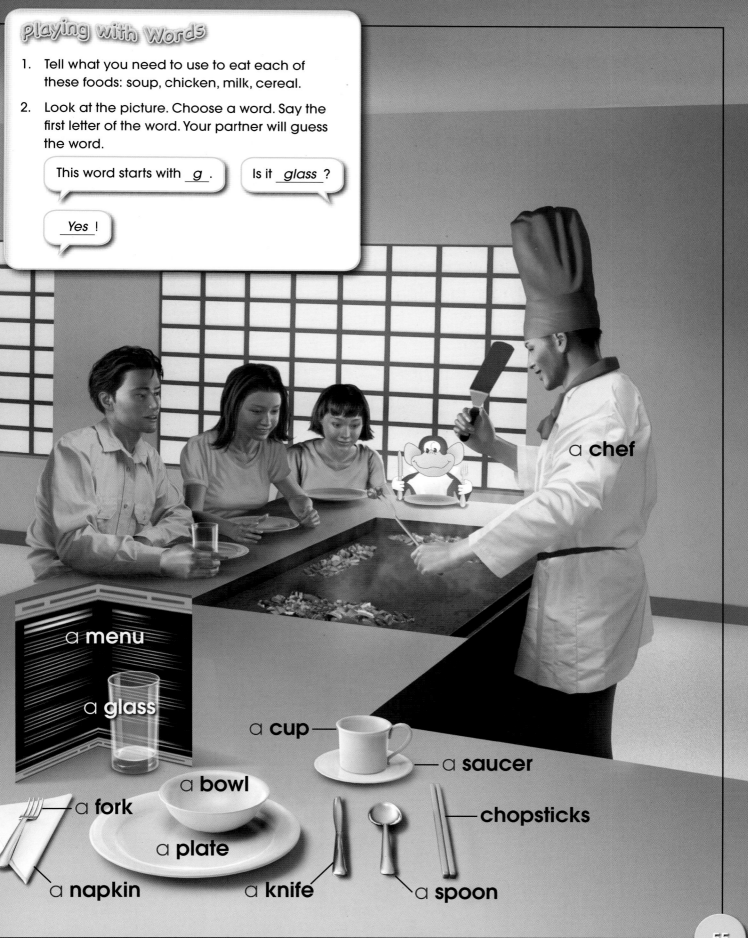

a chef

a menu

a glass

a cup

a saucer

a bowl

a fork

chopsticks

a plate

a napkin

a knife

a spoon

MAIN ST
OAK AVE

Rhyme Time

I'm at the **daycare center** with my mother.

We came to pick up my little brother.

But where is he? I don't see Jim.

I really wish I could find him.

He isn't sleeping in the **crib.**

That's not him wearing the **bib.**

He isn't sitting in the **high chair.**

Oh Mommy, look! I see him there!

He's all dressed up like a bear!

a **playpen**

a **diaper**

a **baby**

baby wipes

a **potty chair**

a crib

a high chair

a bib

a bottle

a parent

a child

a stroller

a pacifier

a rattle

57

At the Construction Site

Rhyme Time

Here are some questions about a **construction site.**

Let's see how many you get right.

What machine can **dig** a hole? Do you know?

The best thing to use is a **backhoe.**

How can you lift heavy things with a chain?

That's not hard. Just use a **crane.**

What can push and move dirt away?

Use a **bulldozer.** That's the best way!

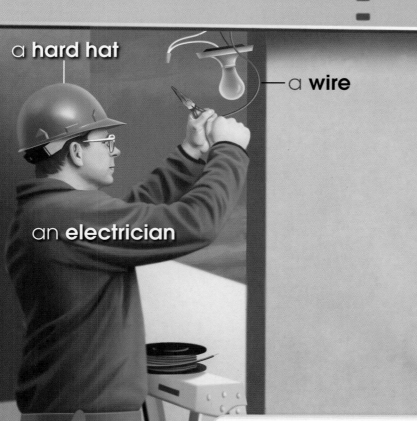

a **hard hat**

— a **wire**

an **electrician**

a **crane**

a **carpenter**

— a **hammer**

a **saw** —

Playing with Words

1. Look at the words. Make 3 lists:
   - people
   - things people drive
   - things people use

2. Which words for people end with the letters *er*? (Hint: There are 2.)

a bulldozer

measure

a backhoe

saw

hammer

a dump truck

dig

a shovel

a pipe

a plumber

climb

59

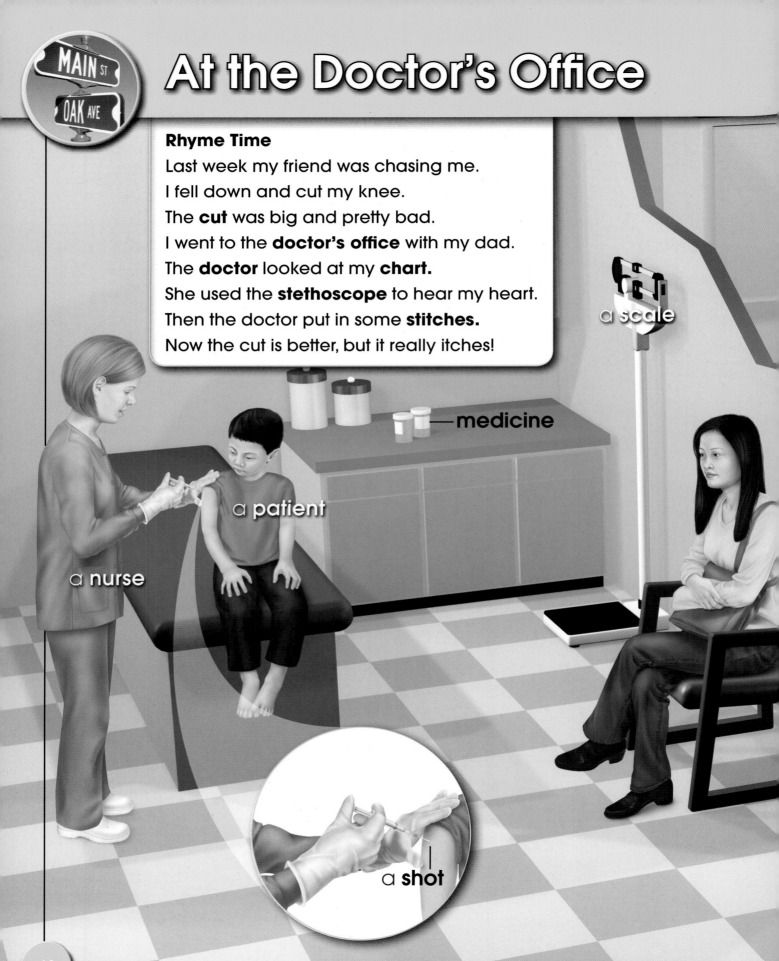

At the Doctor's Office

Rhyme Time

Last week my friend was chasing me.

I fell down and cut my knee.

The **cut** was big and pretty bad.

I went to the **doctor's office** with my dad.

The **doctor** looked at my **chart.**

She used the **stethoscope** to hear my heart.

Then the doctor put in some **stitches.**

Now the cut is better, but it really itches!

a scale

medicine

a patient

a nurse

a **shot**

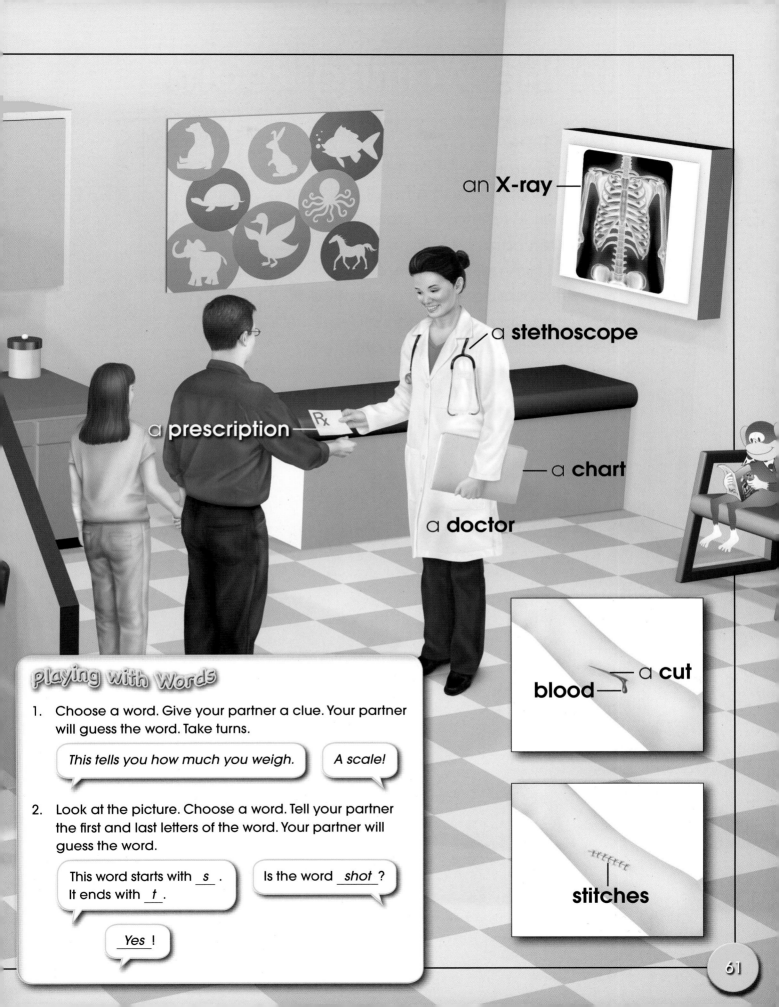

an **X-ray**

a **stethoscope**

a **prescription**

a **chart**

a **doctor**

blood — a **cut**

stitches

61

In the Waiting Room

Rhyme Time

How did Kumar get a **bump?**
He fell out of bed with a great big "thump!"
Why does Kwan have a **stomachache?**
He ate ten candy bars and a big cake.
Why did Tum get a **sore throat?**
She went outside without a warm coat.
Why does Elisa **sneeze** and sneeze?
It's all because of the grass and trees.

a **fever**

an **earache**

a **sore throat**

tissues

a **stomachache**

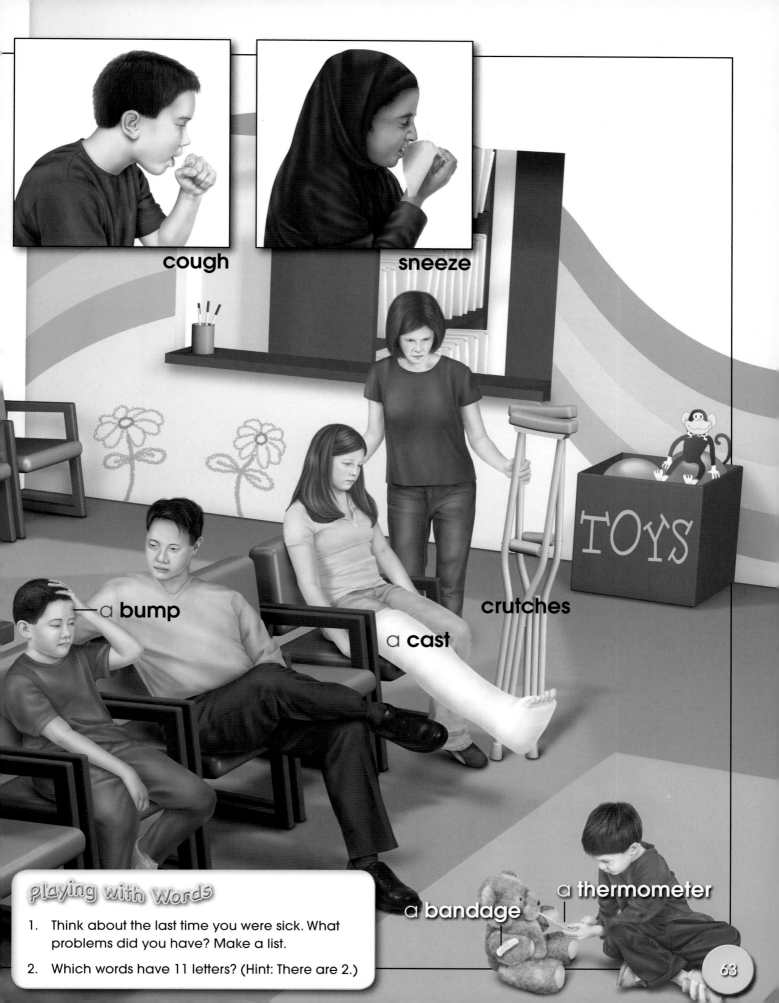

cough

sneeze

a bump

crutches

a cast

TOYS

a thermometer

a bandage

playing with Words

1. Think about the last time you were sick. What problems did you have? Make a list.

2. Which words have 11 letters? (Hint: There are 2.)

63

Jobs

Rhyme Time

There are so many things I'd like to be.

Maybe I'll have two **jobs,** or even three.

I'd like to be a **pilot**

and fly up in the sky.

I could be a **baker**

and make bread and pies.

Or maybe I'll be a **carpenter**

who makes bookshelves and beds

or a **firefighter** who drives

a big fire truck that's red.

a **painter**

an **actor**

a **police officer**

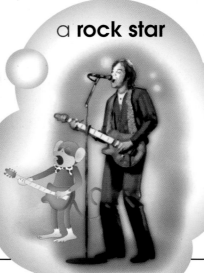

a **rock star**

a **firefighter**

64

a **scientist**

a **carpenter**

a **hairstylist**

a **pilot**

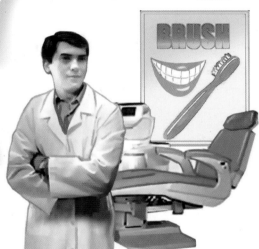

a **baker**

a **truck driver**

a **dentist**

a **plumber**

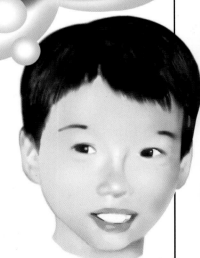

In My Classroom

Rhyme Time

Here are some questions to think about.

I bet you'll be able to figure them out.

What is round, has numbers, and says tick-tock?

That's right. Of course, it is a **clock.**

You write on the **board** with this. It's often white.

Good job. It's **chalk.** You are right.

This holds your books. You wear it on your back.

That's right. You guessed it. It is a **backpack.**

I have no more questions. You've answered each one.

You did a great job! Now this rhyme is done.

a **board**

chalk

an **eraser**

a **teacher**

a **globe**

a **wastebasket**

Playing with Words

1. Look at the words. Make 2 lists:
    *   things that are a circle
    *   things that are a rectangle

2. Practice this conversation.

    Is there _a globe_ in our classroom?

    Yes, there is. / No, there isn't.

 a **clock**

the **alphabet**

Aa Bb Cc Dd Ee Ff Gg Hh Ii Jj Kk Ll Mm Nn Oo Pp Qq Rr Ss Tt Uu Vv Ww Xx Yy Z

a **poster**

a **backpack**

 a **student**

 a **map**

a **chair**

a **desk**

Read, Write, Spell

Rhyme Time

What I Like to Do in Class:

Build towers with blocks.

Look at rocks.

Count to ten.

Write with a pen.

Spell my name.

Play lots of games.

Talk with friends

when school ends.

look at

build

think

count

1 . . . 2 . . . 3 . . . 4

sit down

stand up

In My Schoolbag

Rhyme Time

I emptied my **schoolbag** on the floor.
There was a **binder, paper,** some **money,** and more.
There were **notebooks, rulers,** a **pencil case,**
a **textbook,** a **stapler,** and an **eraser** to erase.
Mom said, "I know you need **pencils** and **pens.**
But I don't understand. Why do you need ten?"

paper

a binder

money

a stapler

a calculator

a textbook

SCIENCE

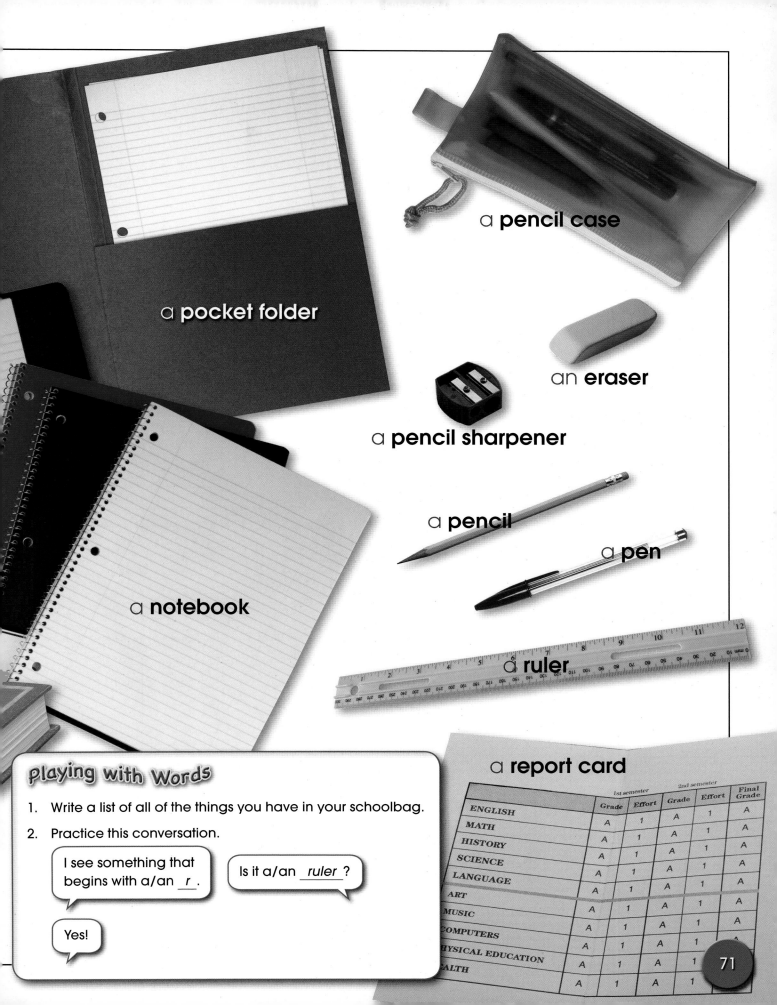

a **pocket folder**

a **pencil case**

an **eraser**

a **pencil sharpener**

a **pencil**

a **pen**

a **notebook**

a **ruler**

a **report card**

	1st semester		2nd semester		Final Grade
	Grade	Effort	Grade	Effort	
ENGLISH	A	1	A	1	A
MATH	A	1	A	1	A
HISTORY	A	1	A	1	A
SCIENCE	A	1	A	1	A
LANGUAGE	A	1	A	1	A
ART	A	1	A	1	A
MUSIC	A	1	A	1	A
COMPUTERS	A	1	A	1	A
PHYSICAL EDUCATION	A	1	A	1	A
HEALTH	A	1	A	1	

playing with Words

1. Write a list of all of the things you have in your schoolbag.
2. Practice this conversation.

> I see something that begins with a/an _r_ .

> Is it a/an _ruler_ ?

> Yes!

Arts and Crafts

How to Make a Butterfly Puppet

1. **Draw** a butterfly on **construction paper.**
2. **Color** it with **crayons** or **markers.**
3. **Cut** out the butterfly.
4. Cut two short pieces of **pipe cleaners** and put them on the top of a **craft stick** with **tape.**
5. **Glue** the butterfly to the craft stick.
6. Let it dry.

draw

color

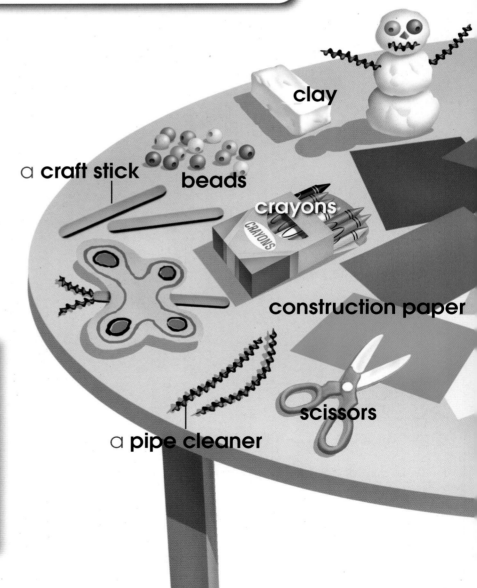

clay

a **craft stick**

beads

crayons

construction paper

a **pipe cleaner**

scissors

paint

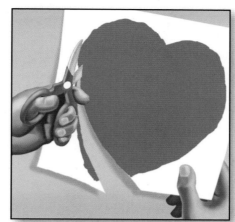

cut

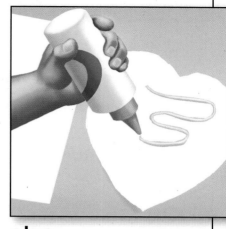

glue

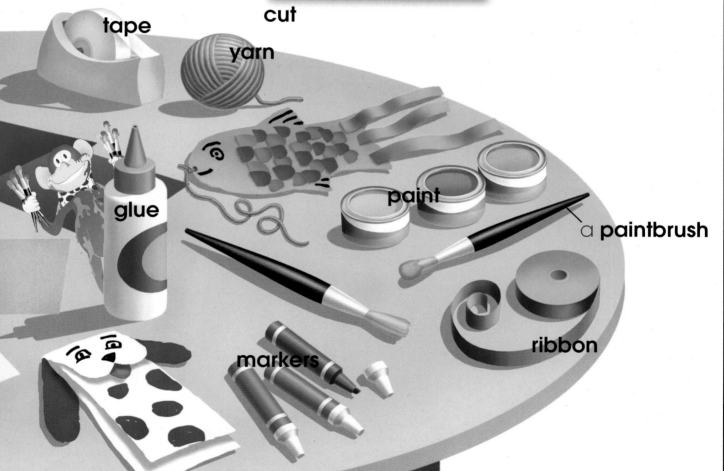

tape

yarn

glue

paint

a **paintbrush**

markers

ribbon

playing with Words

1. Look at the dog, the butterfly, the fish, and the snowman in the picture. What things do you need to make each project?

2. Practice this conversation.

> Can I have the _beads_ ?

> Sure. Can you please pass me the _glue_ ?

Musical Instruments

Rhyme Time

Welcome to **music** class. Please come in!
Now that you're here, we can begin.
Rum-pa-pum-pum.
Do you hear the **drum?**
Toot-toot-toot.
That's the **flute.**
Hear the **triangle** ring
with a ting-a-ling-ling.
Choose an **instrument** you'd like to play.
I'll teach you to use it. We'll start today.

a **saxophone**

a **harmonica**

a **xylophone**

a **guitar**

an **accordion**

castanets

cymbals

a trumpet

a tuba

a piano

a flute

a drum

a triangle

a recorder

a tambourine

a violin

playing with Words

1. Choose an instrument. Pretend to play it. Your class will guess the instrument. Take turns.

2. Which word begins with an *r* and ends with an *r*? Which word begins with a *t* and ends with a *t*?

75

Fruit

Fun Facts

- **Strawberries** are the only **fruit** that have their seeds on the outside.
- **Lemons** have more sugar than strawberries.
- **Orange** trees first grew in China.
- **Bananas** and **mangoes** are the most popular fruit in the world.
- **Raisins** are dried **grapes.**

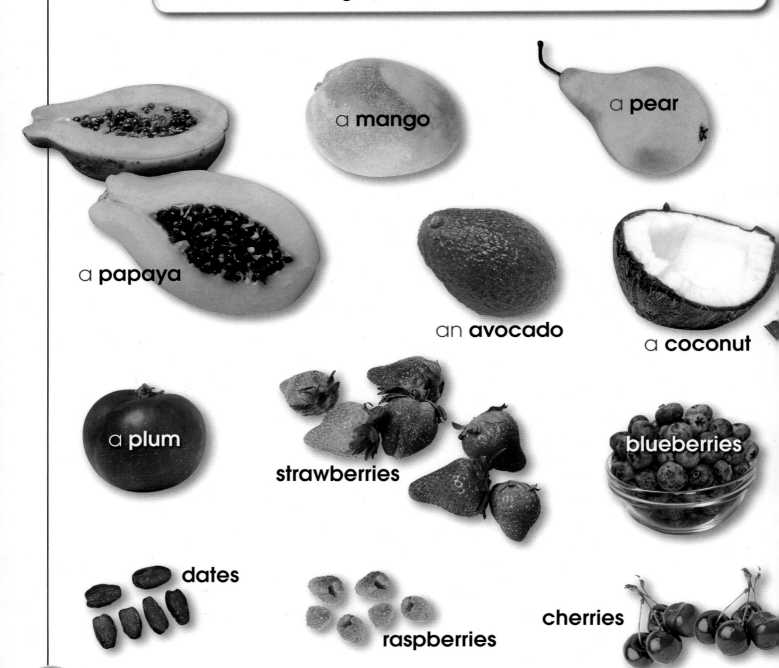

a **papaya**

a **mango**

a **pear**

an **avocado**

a **coconut**

a **plum**

strawberries

blueberries

dates

raspberries

cherries

a melon

a pineapple

a kiwi

a lemon

a peach

an orange

an apple

a banana

raisins

grapes

77

Vegetables

Rhyme Time

I made **vegetable** soup with my dad.

The soup is finished, and it's really not bad!

We chopped **onions, carrots,** and **potatoes.**

We cooked them with **mushrooms** and **tomatoes.**

We added a **chili** and **corn** and **peas.**

I'll give you some, if you just say "please."

a **chili**

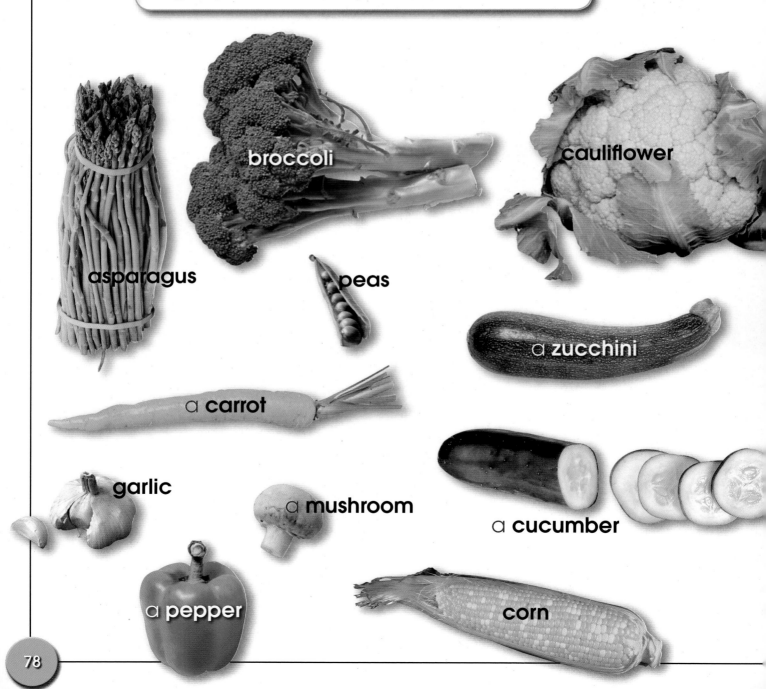

asparagus

broccoli

cauliflower

peas

a **zucchini**

a **carrot**

garlic

a **mushroom**

a **cucumber**

a **pepper**

corn

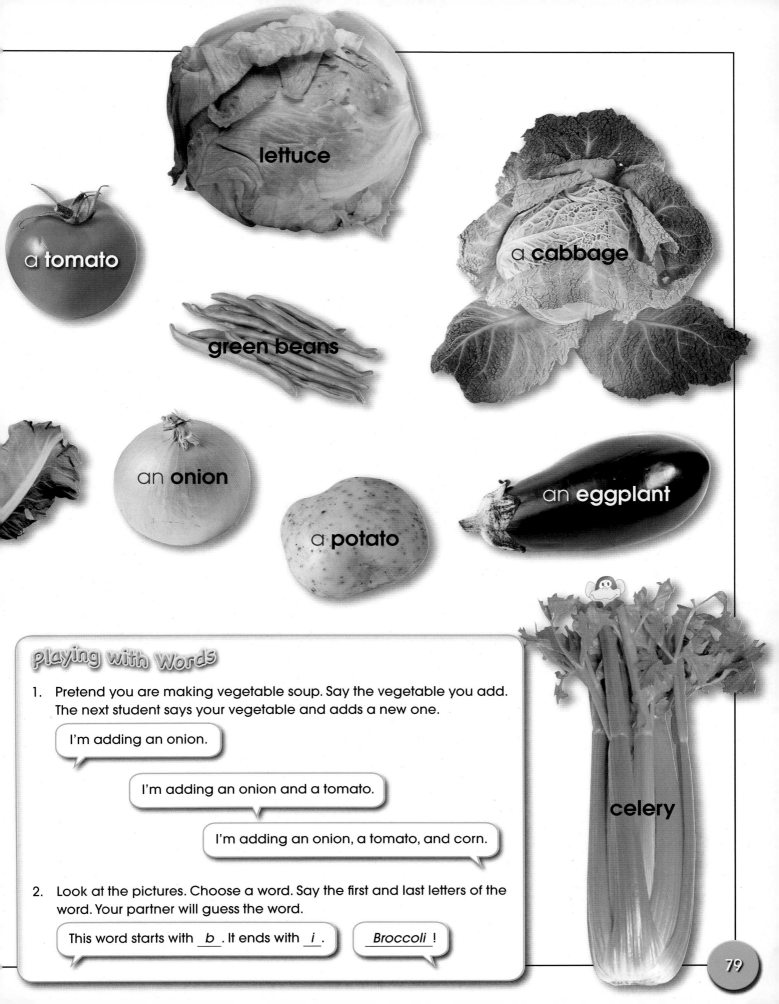

lettuce

a cabbage

a tomato

green beans

an onion

a potato

an eggplant

celery

Playing with Words

1. Pretend you are making vegetable soup. Say the vegetable you add. The next student says your vegetable and adds a new one.

   I'm adding an onion.

   I'm adding an onion and a tomato.

   I'm adding an onion, a tomato, and corn.

2. Look at the pictures. Choose a word. Say the first and last letters of the word. Your partner will guess the word.

   This word starts with _b_ . It ends with _i_ .

   Broccoli !

Food 1

Fun Facts

- Most people eat over 1,000 pounds of **food** a year!
- Most **rice** is grown under water.
- It takes 12 honeybees to make 1 tablespoon of **honey.**
- It takes about 10 pounds of milk to make 1 pound of **cheese.**
- Brazil makes more **sugar** than any country in the world.

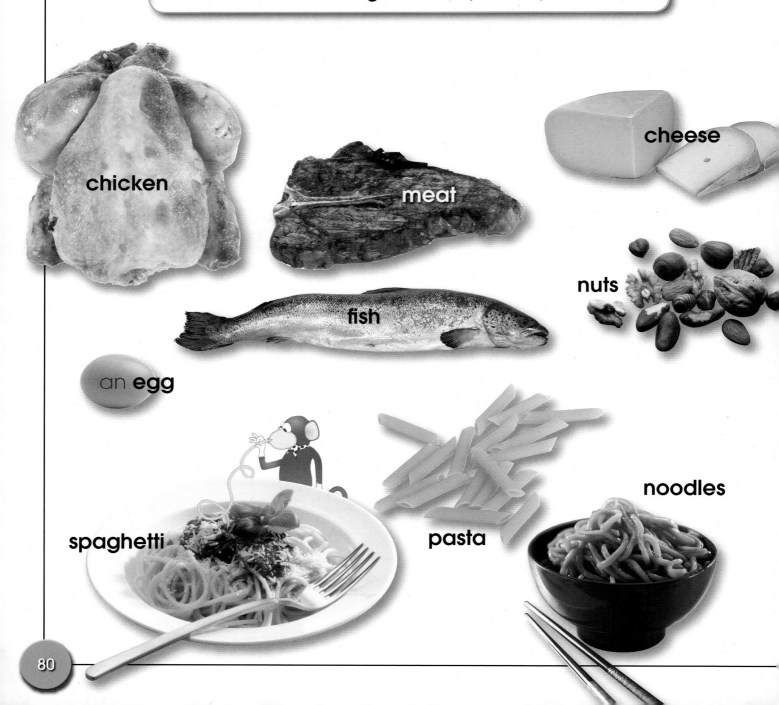

chicken

meat

cheese

nuts

fish

an **egg**

spaghetti

pasta

noodles

sugar

honey

jam

pepper

salt

butter

salad

soup

bread

rice

beans

cereal

1. What are your three favorite foods here? Ask your partner his or her three favorites. Do you and your partner have any of the same favorites?

2. Find the long *e* sound in these words: *bean, meat, cheese.* Which letters make the long *e* sound in each word?

81

Food 2

Fun Facts

- You can live without **food** for about a month.
  You can only live without **water** for about a week.
- One cow can give 200,000 glasses of **milk** in its life.
- The average person eats 12 pounds of **chocolate** a year.
- The average American child eats about 46 slices of **pizza** a year.
- It takes about 50 licks to finish one scoop of **ice cream.**

a **sandwich**

an **egg roll**

a **hamburger**

french fries

a **taco**

sushi

a **pizza**

a **kebab**

water

juice

milk

soda

tea

coffee

ice cream —

a **pie**

a **cookie**

Playing with Words

1. Look at the words. Make 3 lists:
   - foods
   - desserts
   - drinks

2. Which word begins with the letters *ch*?
   Which word ends with the letters *ch*?

chocolate

Story Time 1

Rhyme Time

Once upon a time there was a **king** and **queen.**

They had the most beautiful daughter you've ever seen.

This **princess** was sad because she lived in a **tower.**

She was bored. She did nothing hour after hour.

Then one day she met a tall and very handsome **prince.**

They got married and have been happy ever since.

a **carriage**

a **fairy godmother**

a **magic wand**

Playing with Words

1. Look at the words. Make 2 lists:
   - people in stories
   - things in stories

2. Look at the picture. Choose a word. Tell your partner the first and last letters of the word. Your partner will guess the word.

This word starts with _c_ . It ends with _n_ .

Is the word _crown_ ?

Yes !

a flag

a princess

a castle

a tower

a throne

a crown

a king

a queen

a prince

Story Time 2

Rhyme Time

Deep in the **forest** there is a **treasure chest.**
It's guarded by a **dragon** who never rests.
But look! Here comes a brave young **knight.**
He's ready to meet the dragon and to fight.
The knight takes out his big, long **sword.**
Soon he will win his reward.

a **giant**

an **elf**

a **wizard**

a **dwarf**

a **genie**

a **magic lamp**

a **flying carpet**

a witch

a broom

a dragon

a forest

a treasure chest

a sword

a fairy

a knight

playing with words

1. Look at the picture. Choose a word. Tell your partner about it. Your partner will guess the word. Take turns.

> It _has wings_ .

> It's _a fairy_ !

2. Which words begin with a *d*? (Hint: There are 2.)
   Which words end with a *d*? (Hint: There are 2.)

Toys and Games

Rhyme Time

My baby brother crawls to my toy box
and throws around my **puzzles** and **blocks.**
I've asked him more than once or twice
not to break my **dolls** or eat my **dice.**
I've tried very hard to explain
that he shouldn't sit on my toy **train.**
He took my **robot.** (It was new.)
He threw it on the floor. It broke in two.
Mom agrees that my toy box
needs a couple of good, strong locks.

a **yo-yo**

a **train**

a **fire truck**

a **computer game**

crayons

a **boat**

a **doll**

a **robot**

a **coloring book**

dice

a board game

a dollhouse

a puzzle

a puppet

a teddy bear

bubbles

an action figure

a dinosaur

a monster

a comic book

SUPER DOG

Playing with Words

1. Look at the toys. Make a list of your 5 favorite toys.

2. Practice this conversation.

> Can I please play with your _blocks_?

> Sure.

> Thanks!

blocks

89

Birthday Party

Rhyme Time

Last week I turned eight.

My **birthday party** was really great.

There were lots of **friends, presents,** and **balloons.**

We ate **potato chips** and **candy** all afternoon.

Then I blew out the **candles** on my **cake.**

I ate three slices. That was a mistake.

Then I finished with a few **cupcakes.**

I had lots of fun, but I got a stomachache!

a **balloon**

wrap

bake

light

blow out

popcorn

a **candle**

an **invitation**

potato chips

a **cupcake**

a **cake**

candy

90

a lollipop

wrapping paper

a bow

a card

friends

a present

Playing with Words

1. Pretend you are planning your next birthday party. How many candles will there be? What kind of cake will you have? What gifts would you like? What food will you eat? Tell your partner.

2. Look at the picture. Choose a word. Tell your partner the first and last letter of the word. Your partner will guess the word. Take turns.

> This word starts with _f_ . It ends with _s_ .

> Is the word _friends_ ?

> _Yes_ !

91

At the Beach

Rhyme Time

When we go to the **beach** there's a lot we bring.
Here are just a few important things.
I need a **shovel** and **pail** so I can dig
and make **sandcastles** that are really big.
My father really likes to swim,
so we bring **flippers** and a **snorkel** for him.
Mom brings a **surfboard,** and also a **beach chair** to relax.
And we bring a **cooler** with lots of snacks!

a **kite**

a **sun hat**

a **beach ball**

a **cooler**

sunscreen

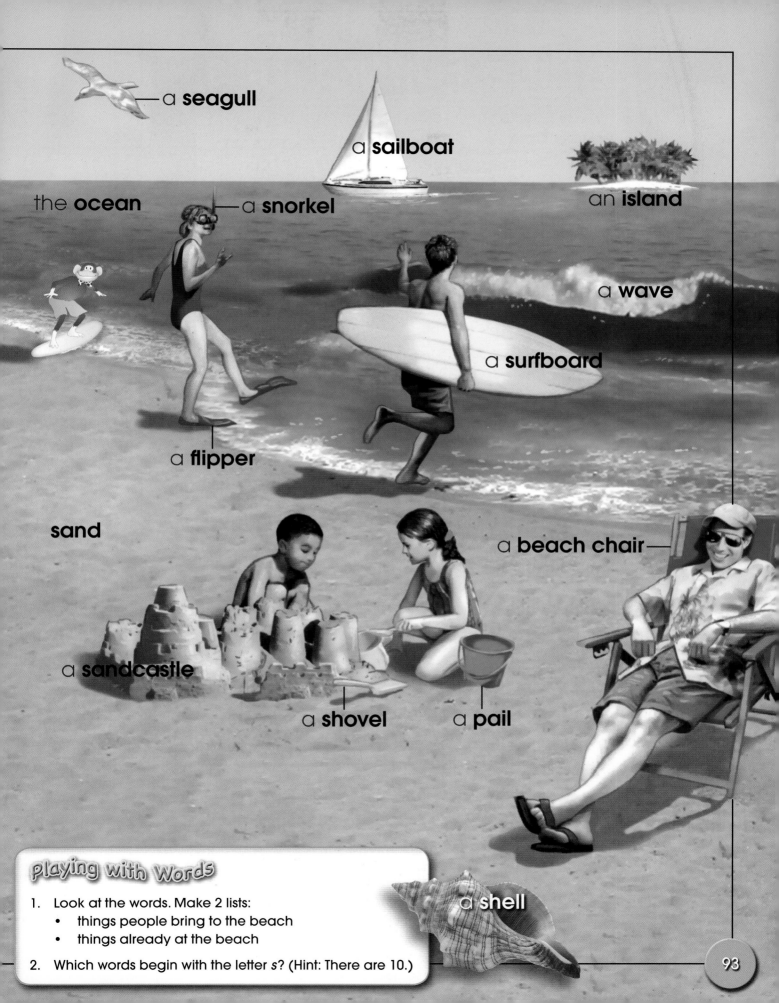

a **seagull**

a **sailboat**

an **island**

the **ocean**

a **snorkel**

a **wave**

a **surfboard**

a **flipper**

sand

a **beach chair**

a **sandcastle**

a **shovel**

a **pail**

Playing with Words

1. Look at the words. Make 2 lists:
   * things people bring to the beach
   * things already at the beach

2. Which words begin with the letter *s*? (Hint: There are 10.)

a **shell**

At the Fairgrounds

Rhyme Time

I love everything at the **fairgrounds,**

like the **carousel** that spins around and around.

When I'm high up on the **Ferris wheel,**

I'm excited and happy. That's how I feel.

I like the **jugglers** and the flying **trapeze.**

Oh can we go to the fairgrounds, please?

fireworks

a **Ferris wheel**

a **roller coaster**

a **carousel**

a **carnival**

TICKETS

a **ticket**

94

playing with words

1. Look at the words. Make 2 lists:
   - people
   - rides

2. Which words have double letters?
   (Hint: There are 4.)
   Example: ju**gg**ler

a **tightrope walker**

a **trapeze**

an **acrobat**

a **lion tamer**

a **circus**

cotton candy

a **juggler**

a **clown**

COTTON CANDY

At the Street Fair

Rhyme Time

Something special happens once each year:

My town has a great **street fair.**

There are **dancers,** and **singers,** and many **musicians.**

There's even a **puppet show** and a **magician.**

Every year on this day in spring,

we **dance,** we **clap,** we laugh and **sing.**

The fun continues all day long.

This year won't you come along?

a dancer

a musician

a singer

a puppet show

a photographer

a camera

a **magician**

an **artist**

a **painting**

play a guitar

sing

clap

dance

take a picture

paint

Playing with Words

1. Look at the words. Make 3 lists:
   - people
   - things
   - actions

2. Look at the picture. Choose a word. Tell your partner the first and last letters of the word. Your partner will guess the word.

> This word starts with _p_ .
> It ends with _r_ .

> Is the word _photographer_ ?

> _Yes_ !

On the Farm

Rhyme Time

The day starts early on the **farm.**
The **rooster**'s crow is like an alarm.
The **farmer** jumps up and gets out of bed.
Soon he's showered, dressed, and fed.
The **chickens** and **pigs** want their breakfast too.
(A **goat** even starts to eat the farmer's shoe!)
He feeds his animals corn and **hay,**
then gets on his **tractor** and drives away.

a **scarecrow**

hay

a **horse**

a **lamb**

a **sheep**

a **goat**

a **chicken**

a **chick**

a **rooster**

a barn

a farmer

a tractor

a bull

a cow

a calf

a donkey

a turkey

a pig

a piglet

Playing with Words

1. Make the sound of one of the animals. Your partner will guess the animal. Take turns.

2. Which words have 3 letters? (Hint: There are 3.)

99

Camping

Rhyme Time

You're going **camping!** There's so much to bring.
Let me remind you about a few things.
Are you going to camp out all night?
Then you need a **tent,** a **sleeping bag,** and a **flashlight.**
Are you going on the **river?** Then bring a **raft** or **canoe.**
And please don't forget to bring a **life jacket,** too.
But the most important things to remember from this rhyme
are to stay safe and have a good time.

a fishing pole

a trailer

a tent

a sleeping bag

matches

a flashlight

a campfire

a mountain

a waterfall

—a trail

a river

a canoe

a raft

—a life jacket

a rope

north

west · east

south

a compass

101

playing with Words

1. Look at the words. Make 2 lists:
   • things you use on the water
   • things you use on land

2. Which words are made of two smaller words?
   (Hint: There are 6.)
   Examples: <u>campfire</u>, <u>fishing</u> <u>pole</u>

Sports

Rhyme Time
Give me a **bat.** Give me a **glove.**
Baseball is the game I love.
I've got my **racket.** There is the **net.**
Are you ready to play **tennis** yet?
Come on. Let's go **rollerblading.**
Hurry, please. I'm tired of waiting.

a **hockey stick**

a **hockey puck**

hockey

a **bat**

a **glove**

a **baseball**

baseball

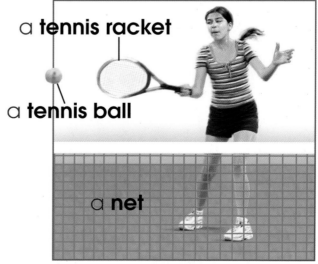

a **tennis racket**

a **tennis ball**

a **net**

tennis

a **rollerblade**

rollerblading

a **hoop**

a **basketball**

basketball

a **goal**

a soccer ball

soccer

karate

Spring

Rhyme Time

What is your favorite season?
Mine is **spring.**
I love the **warm** weather
and the **rainy** days it brings.
I splash in the **puddles**
and **dig** in the **mud.**
I **plant** pretty **flowers**
and smile at the first **bud.**

a flower

a bud—

a stem—

a leaf—

a root—

dig

plant

water

a garden

—a watering can

seeds

mud

a puddle

a rainbow

a cloud

It's **cloudy!**

It's **rainy!**

rain

a **bush**

a **lawn mower**

grass

°F °C
140 — 60
120 — 50
100 — 40
80 — 30
60 — 20
40 — 10
20 — 0±
±0 — 10
20 — 20
20 — 30
40 — 40

warm

Playing with Words

1. Choose something in the picture. Tell your partner about it. Your partner will guess the word. Take turns.

   It is green. You can walk on it.   *Grass!*

2. Your partner will point to something in the picture. Say the word. Try to spell the word. Take turns.

Summer

a fan

Rhyme Time

It's time for long, **hot summer** days
with nothing to do but laugh and play.
No more homework and no more school.
It's time to **splash** and **swim** in the **pool.**
Hang up your jacket and put away your boots.
It's time for **sunglasses** and **bathing suits.**
We're going to laugh and play in the **sun.**
We're going to have so much fun!

water wings

a **pool**

sunglasses

watermelon

a **barbecue grill**

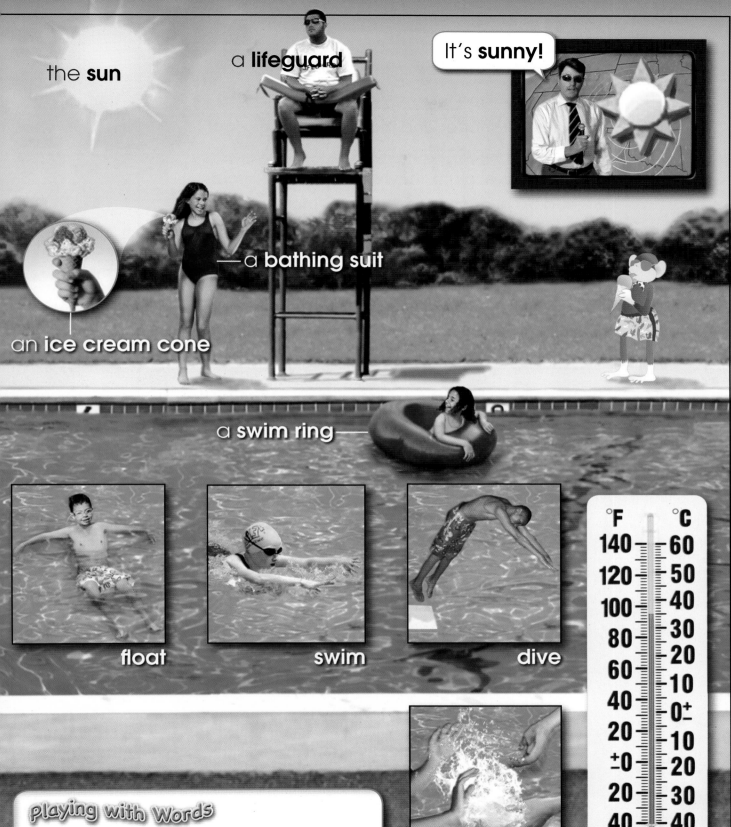

the **sun**

a **lifeguard**

It's **sunny!**

an **ice cream cone**

— a **bathing suit**

a **swim ring** —

float

swim

dive

splash

hot

°F 140 120 100 80 60 40 20 ±0 20 40

°C 60 50 40 30 20 10 0± 10 20 30 40

Playing with Words

1. Choose a word. Draw a picture of it. Your partner will guess the word. Take turns.

2. Choose a word. Say how many letters there are in your word. Your partner will guess the word. Take turns.

107

Fall

Rhyme Time

The days get shorter and the weather turns **cool.**
Children are ready to go back to school.
On one special night, they walk down the street.
Dressed up in **costumes** they say, "Trick or treat!"
Leaves fall from the **trees** and cover the ground.
The **wind** blows the leaves around and around.
Soon they'll be gone—leaves of orange, gold, and red.
It is getting colder. Winter is ahead.

a **wheelbarrow**

a **pile**

—a **rake**

—a **broom**

sweep

rake

Playing with Words

1. Look at the picture. Choose a word. Draw a picture of it. Your partner will guess the word. Take turns.

2. Which words have *ee* in them? (Hint: There are 3.) What sound does *ee* make?

It's **windy!**

wind

a **tree**

a **school bus**

a **leaf**

a **costume**

ride a **bike**

skateboard

a **pumpkin**

cool

109

Winter

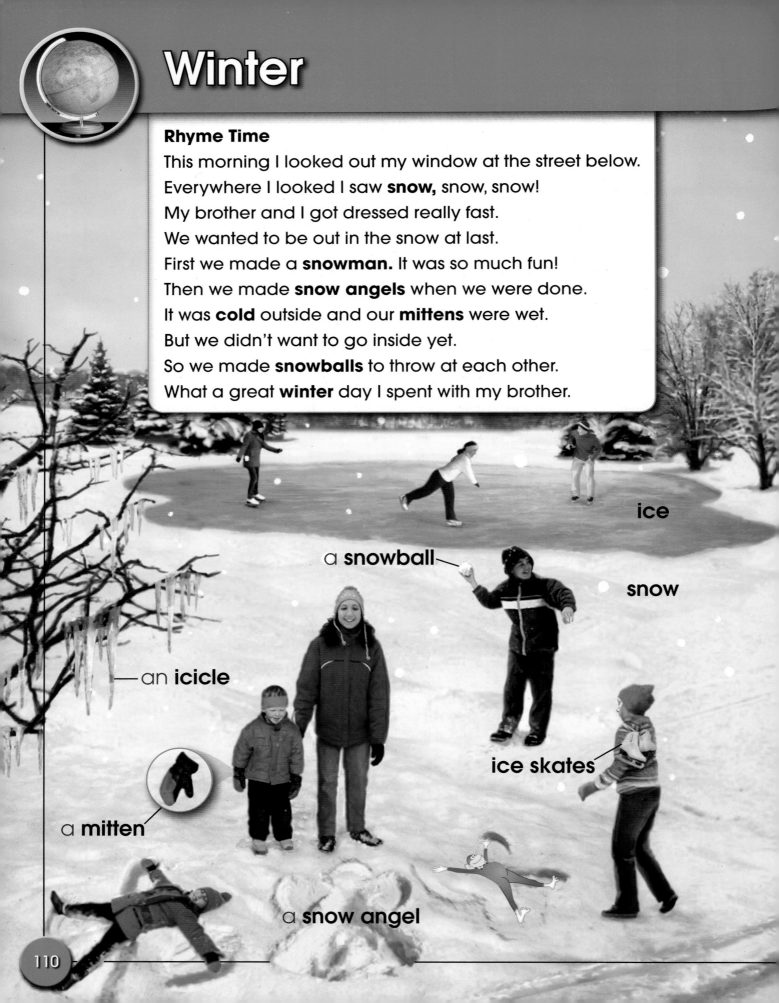

Rhyme Time

This morning I looked out my window at the street below.

Everywhere I looked I saw **snow,** snow, snow!

My brother and I got dressed really fast.

We wanted to be out in the snow at last.

First we made a **snowman.** It was so much fun!

Then we made **snow angels** when we were done.

It was **cold** outside and our **mittens** were wet.

But we didn't want to go inside yet.

So we made **snowballs** to throw at each other.

What a great **winter** day I spent with my brother.

ice

a **snowball**

snow

an **icicle**

ice skates

a **mitten**

a **snow angel**

It's **snowing!**

a **snowflake**

a **Christmas tree**

Santa Claus

a **sled**

a **snowboard**

cold

skis

a **snowman**

playing with Words

1. Pretend today is a snowy day. What will you do? Tell your partner.

2. Find the words that have "snow" in them. (Hint: There are 6.)

111

Bugs

an **ant**

a **bee**

a **beetle**

a **butterfly**

a **cricket**

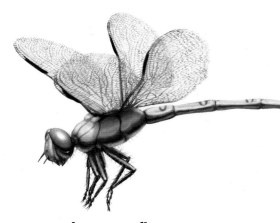

a **dragonfly**

a **centipede**

a **fly**

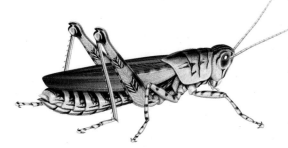

a **grasshopper**

a **caterpillar** → a **cocoon** → a **moth**

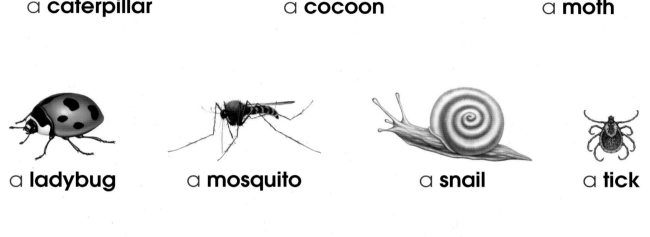

a **ladybug**   a **mosquito**   a **snail**   a **tick**

a **wasp**

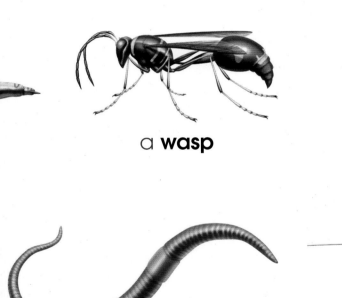

a **worm**

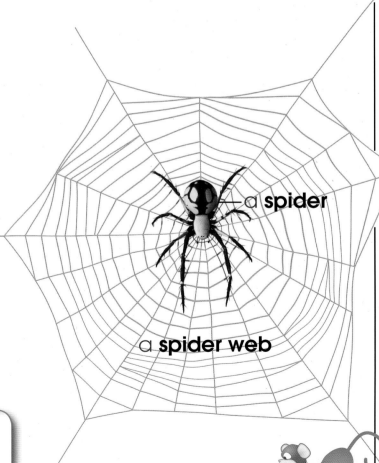

a **spider**

a **spider web**

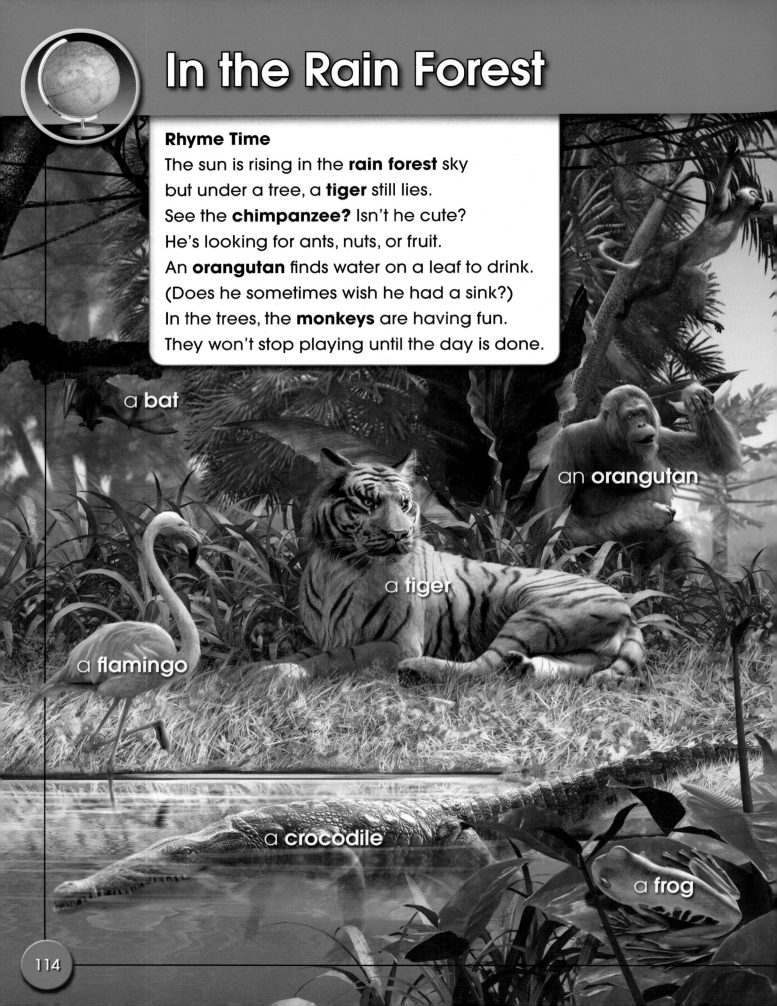

In the Rain Forest

Rhyme Time

The sun is rising in the **rain forest** sky
but under a tree, a **tiger** still lies.
See the **chimpanzee?** Isn't he cute?
He's looking for ants, nuts, or fruit.
An **orangutan** finds water on a leaf to drink.
(Does he sometimes wish he had a sink?)
In the trees, the **monkeys** are having fun.
They won't stop playing until the day is done.

a **bat**

an **orangutan**

a **flamingo**

a **tiger**

a **crocodile**

a **frog**

a parrot

a monkey

a feather

a wing

a beak

a gorilla

a peacock

a chimpanzee

a hummingbird

Playing with Words

1. Which rain forest animals have fur? (Hint: There are 6.)
   Which have wings? (Hint: There are 5.)

2. Which words have long *e* sounds? (Hint: There are 4.)
   Example: beak

115

In the Grasslands

Fun Facts

- **Rhinoceroses** do not eat any meat.
- **Leopards** can leap more than 20 feet.
- **Elephants** put their **trunks** in each other's mouths when they meet.
- **Lions** spend 20 hours a day at rest or asleep.
- **Giraffes** need less than 2 hours sleep.

an **elephant**

an **ostrich**

a **buffalo**

a **hippopotamus**

a **zebra**

spots

stripes

a **horn**

a **tusk**

a **trunk**

a **koala**

a giraffe

a **kangaroo**

a **rhinoceros**

a lion

a **leopard**

Playing with Words

1. Pretend to be one of these animals. Move like the animal. Make the sound of the animal. Your class will guess the name of the animal.

2. Which words end with the letter *a*? (Hint: There are 2.) Make the sound of the letter *a* in those words.

117

In the Sea

Rhyme Time
Sea animals can do amazing things.
Some **whales** can even sing.
Octopuses use their arms to taste and feel.
Sharks can go weeks without a meal.
A hurt **lobster** can grow brand new legs.
A **shrimp** can lay 500,000 eggs!

a **sea horse**

seaweed

a **jellyfish**

a **turtle**

a **coral reef**

a **mussel**

an **octopus**

a **starfish**

a **stingray**

an **oyster**

a **shrimp**

a **pearl**

a **crab**

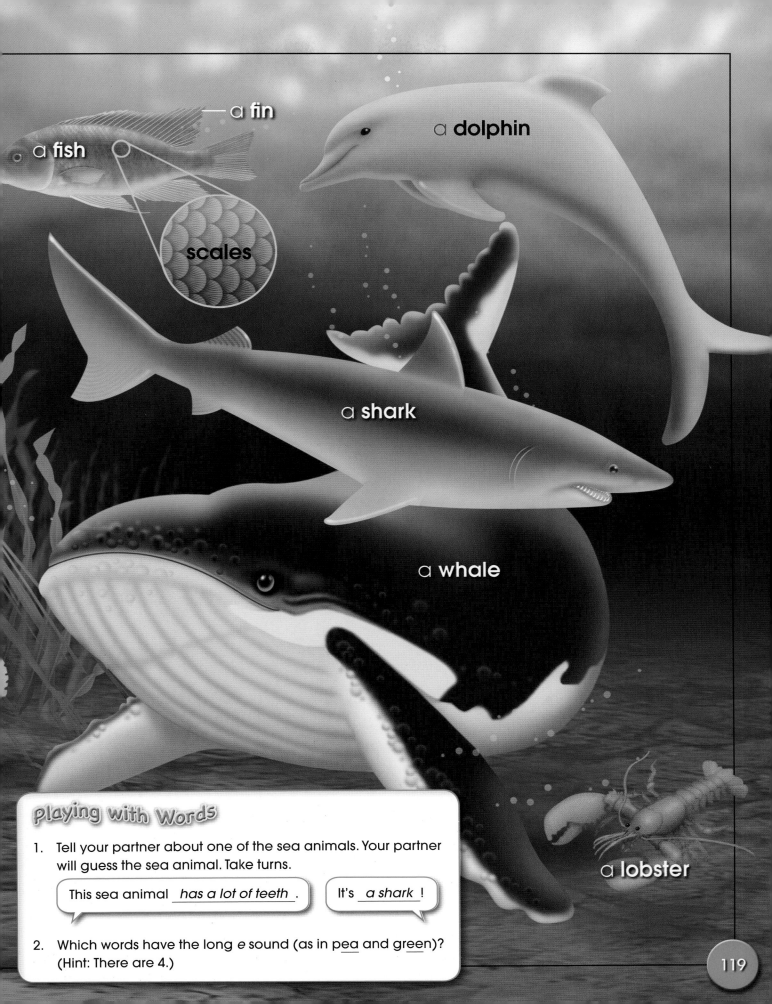

a fish

— a fin

a dolphin

scales

a shark

a whale

a lobster

playing with words

1. Tell your partner about one of the sea animals. Your partner will guess the sea animal. Take turns.

This sea animal _has a lot of teeth_ .

It's _a shark_ !

2. Which words have the long e sound (as in p<u>ea</u> and gr<u>ee</u>n)? (Hint: There are 4.)

In the Woodlands

Rhyme Time

The **woodlands** have many sounds,
some from above and some on the ground.
Listen! A **woodpecker** is making a hole in a tree.
He's looking for insects, like ants and bees.
Up high in a **nest,** a **robin** sings.
In the **pond** below, a **duck** flaps its wings.
If you listen closely, you will hear
a hopping **rabbit** and a running **deer.**

an **eagle**

a **raccoon**

a **skunk**

a **chipmunk**

a **rabbit**

a **mouse**

a squirrel

a robin

a nest

a deer

a duck

a woodpecker

a pond

a beaver

a toad

In the Polar Lands

Fun Facts

- **Reindeer** grow new **antlers** every year.
- Father **penguins** take care of penguin eggs.
- **Seals** can stay underwater for 30 minutes.
- **Polar bears** only weigh a pound when they are born. But when they grow up, they weigh more than 1,000 pounds!

a **lake**

an **igloo**

a **wolf**

an **Eskimo**

a **polar bear**

a **fox**

a **cub**

a **penguin**

a **puffin**

a **seal**

122

an **antler**

a **moose**

a **reindeer**

a **grizzly bear**

a **walrus**

a **flipper**

a **goose**

Playing with Words

1. Which animals have antlers? (Hint: There are 2.)
   Which animals have flippers? (Hint: There are 3.)

2. Which 2 words rhyme?

In the Desert

Rhyme Time

Here in the **desert** it's hot and dry.
Almost no water falls from the sky.
Lizards and **snakes** like to lie in the sun,
but **owls** come out when the day is done.
Where is the water? There isn't much here.
Camels can live without it for weeks, and **tortoises** a year!

an **owl**

a **palm tree**

a **camel**

a **cactus**

an **oasis**

a **rock**

a **coyote**

a **snake**

a **scorpion**

a **lizard**

a vulture

claws

a sand dune

a tortoise

Playing with Words

1. Look at the words. Make 2 lists:
    *   animals you see in the desert
    *   other things you see in the desert

2. Which words have 5 letters?
    (Hint: There are 4.)

Space

Fun Facts

- The **sun** is a **star.**
- The sun is the closest star to **Earth.**
- The **moon** goes around Earth once each day.
- Earth goes around the sun once each year.
- Yuri Gagarin was the first **astronaut** to ride a **rocket** into **space.**

a **constellation**

Neptune

Uranus

a **star**

a **rocket**

a **telescope**

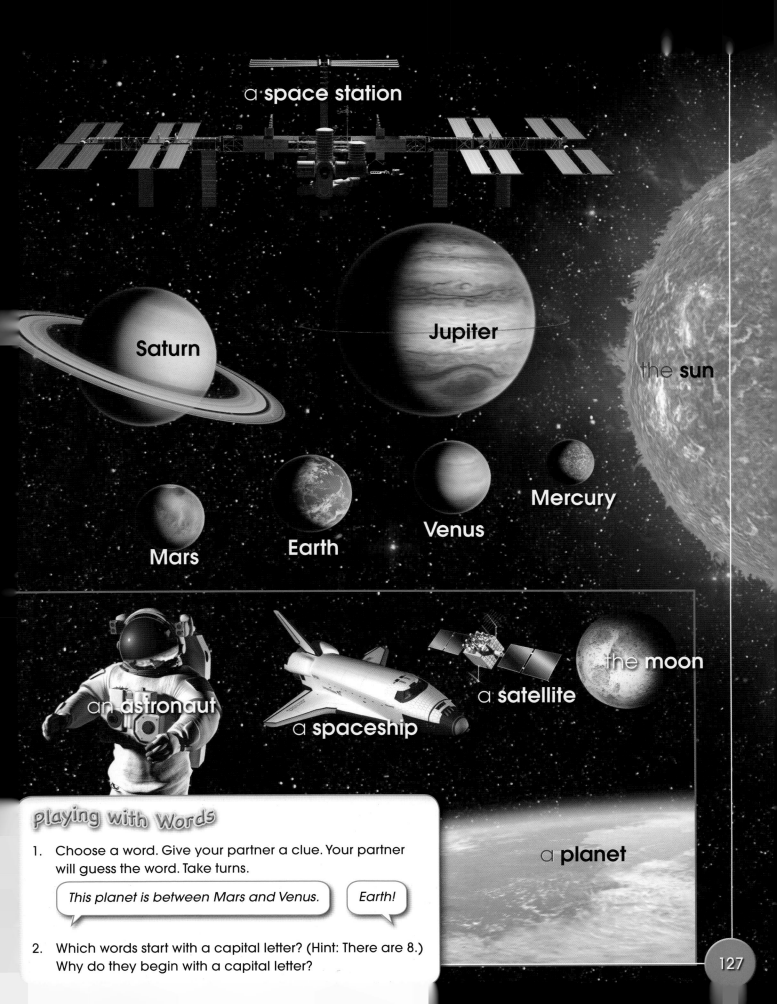

a **space station**

Saturn

Jupiter

the **sun**

Mercury

Venus

Earth

Mars

an **astronaut**

a **spaceship**

a **satellite**

the **moon**

a **planet**

Playing with Words

1. Choose a word. Give your partner a clue. Your partner will guess the word. Take turns.

   This planet is between Mars and Venus.   *Earth!*

2. Which words start with a capital letter? (Hint: There are 8.) Why do they begin with a capital letter?

127

Alphabetical Word List

Verb and verb phrase entries appear in *italics*. Some words appear twice in the word list: once in italics and once in regular type. In these cases, the italicized entry is a verb, and the regular type entry is a noun.

Thematic Word List

Letters
pages 2–3
ant
apple
bird
boy
cake
cat
dinosaur
dog
egg
elephant
fly
frog
gift
girl
horse
house
ice cream
igloo
jellyfish
jump rope
kangaroo
kite
leaf
lion
man
mouse
necklace
nut
orange
owl
pencil
pig
queen
quilt
rabbit
rainbow
seal
strawberry
train
tree
umbrella
unicorn
violin
volcano
wagon
woman
X-ray
xylophone
yarn
yo-yo
zebra
zipper

Numbers
pages 4–5
one
two
three
four
five
six
seven
eight
nine
ten
eleven
twelve
thirteen
fourteen
fifteen
sixteen
seventeen
eighteen
nineteen
twenty
first
second
third
fourth
fifth
plus
minus
equals

Colors and Shapes
pages 6–7
circle
heart
rectangle
square
star
triangle
black
blue
brown
gray
green
orange
pink
purple
red
white
yellow

In, On, Over
pages 8–9
above
across from
around
behind
below
between
down
in
in front of
next to
on
on the left of
on the right of
over
through
under
up

Opposites
pages 10–11
big
clean
closed
dirty
fast
long
loud
new
old
open
quiet
short
slow
small
tall
young

Time
pages 12–13
calendar
day
month
week
January
February
March
April
May
June
July
August
September
October
November
December
afternoon
evening
hour
minute
morning
night
clock
watch
1:00/one o-clock
1:15/one fifteen
1:30/one thirty
1:45/one forty-five

Face and Hair
pages 14–15
braces
cheek
chin
ear
eye
eyebrow
forehead
glasses
hair
mouth
nose
tongue
tooth
braid
curly
long
pigtail
ponytail
short
straight

Body
pages 16–17
ankle
arm
back
chest
elbow
finger
foot
hand
head
heel
knee
leg
neck
shoulder
stomach
thumb
toe
wrist

Clothes 1
pages 18–19
belt
blouse
bracelet
earrings
jacket
jeans
jewelry
necklace
ring
shorts
skirt
sneaker
sweatshirt

tights
T-shirt
underpants
undershirt
underwear

Clothes 2
pages 20–21
baseball cap
boot
button
coat
collar
dress
glove
hat
pants
pocket
raincoat
sandal
scarf
shirt
shoe
sleeve
sock
sweater
tie
umbrella

My Family
pages 22–23
aunt
brother
cousin
dad
father
grandfather
grandma
grandmother
grandpa
grandparents
me
mom
mother
parents
sister
uncle

Feelings
pages 24–25
cry
drink
eat
happy
hide
hungry
laugh
mad
sad
scared

silly
smile
thirsty
tired
yawn
yell

My Day
pages 26–27
brush my teeth
call my friend
clean my room
come home
do my homework
eat breakfast
eat lunch
eat dinner
get dressed
get up
go to bed
go to school
hug my dad
kiss my mom
make my bed
play with friends
sleep
take a shower
watch TV

In the Kitchen
pages 28–29
cabinet
cook
counter
drawer
kettle
microwave
oven
pan
pot
refrigerator
stove
toaster
wash the dishes

In the Living Room
pages 30–31
armchair
CD player
ceiling
coffee table
couch
DVD player
earphones
fire
fireplace
floor
lamp
light
picture
plant
rug

telephone
television
vase
wall

In the Bedroom
pages 32–33
alarm clock
bed
blanket
carpet
closet
comforter
curtain
dresser
hanger
lamp
pajamas
pillow
sheet
slipper
stuffed animals
toy box

In the Bathroom
pages 34–35
bath mat
bathtub
brush
comb
flush the toilet
mirror
shampoo
shower
sink
soap
take a bath
take a shower
toilet
toilet paper
toothbrush
toothpaste
towel
wash your hands
washcloth

Outside the House
pages 36–37
address
chimney
door
driveway
fence
gate
helmet
house
key
mail carrier
neighbor
porch
roof
step

tree house
tricycle
wagon
window
yard

In the Garage
pages 38–39
battery
drill
dryer
garbage can
hammer
iron
ladder
lightbulb
nail
paint
paintbrush
saw
screwdriver
tape measure
washing machine
wrench

On the Move
pages 40–41
airplane
airport
bike
bridge
bus
car
ferry
helicopter
hot air balloon
motorcycle
road
sailboat
ship
skateboard
subway
taxi
train
truck
tunnel
van
wheelchair

Around Town
pages 42–43
ambulance
apartment building
bakery
bank
bus stop
crosswalk
factory
fire hydrant
fire station
florist
gas station

134

hospital
laundromat
mailbox
museum
post office
school
street
supermarket
theater
train station

In the Park
pages 44–45
ball
bench
hill
jump rope
kite
monkey bars
path
picnic
playground
sandbox
seesaw
slide
statue
swing
trash can
zoo

Run, Jump, Throw
pages 46–47
catch
chase
climb
fall
hop
jump
kick
pull
push
ride
run
slide
swing
throw

At the Library
pages 48–49
atlas
book
bookshelf
check out
checkout desk
computer
dictionary
DVD
librarian
library card
magazine
newspaper

return
videotape

Pets at the Vet
pages 50–51
bird
bone
cage
cat
collar
dog
fish
fishbowl
fur
kitten
leash
mouse
paw
puppy
tail
turtle
veterinarian

At the Mall
pages 52–53
ATM
bag
bookstore
candy store
cell phone
clothing store
elevator
escalator
food court
movie theater
music store
pet shop
restroom
shoe store
shopper
toy store

At the Restaurant
pages 54–55
bowl
chair
chef
chopsticks
cup
fork
glass
knife
menu
napkin
pass
plate
pour
saucer
serve
spoon
stir

table
tablecloth
waiter

At the Daycare Center
pages 56–57
baby
baby wipes
bib
bottle
child
crib
diaper
high chair
pacifier
parent
playpen
potty chair
rattle
stroller

At the Construction Site
pages 58–59
backhoe
bulldozer
carpenter
climb
crane
dig
dump truck
electrician
hammer
hammer
hard hat
measure
pipe
plumber
saw
saw
shovel
wire

At the Doctor's Office
pages 60–61
blood
chart
cut
doctor
medicine
nurse
patient
prescription
scale
shot
stethoscope
stitches
X-ray

In the Waiting Room
pages 62–63
bandage
bump

cast
cough
crutches
earache
fever
sneeze
sore throat
stomach ache
thermometer
tissues

Jobs
pages 64–65
actor
baker
carpenter
dentist
firefighter
hairstylist
painter
pilot
plumber
police officer
rock star
scientist
truck driver

In My Classroom
pages 66–67
alphabet
backpack
board
chair
chalk
clock
desk
eraser
globe
map
poster
student
teacher
wastebasket

Read, Write, Spell
pages 68–69
build
close
count
give
listen
look at
open
read
sit down
spell
stand up
take
talk
think
write

135

In My Schoolbag
binder
calculator
eraser
money
notebook
paper
pen
pencil
pencil case
pencil sharpener
pocket folder
report card
ruler
stapler
textbook

Arts and Crafts
beads
clay
color
construction paper
craft stick
crayons
cut
draw
glue
glue
markers
paint
paint
paintbrush
pipe cleaner
ribbon
scissors
tape
yarn

Musical Instruments
accordion
castanets
cymbals
drum
flute
guitar
harmonica
piano
recorder
saxophone
tambourine
triangle
trumpet
tuba
violin
xylophone

Fruit
apple
avocado
banana
blueberries
cherries
coconut
dates
grapes
kiwi
lemon
mango
melon
orange
papaya
peach
pear
pineapple
plum
raisins
raspberries
strawberries

Vegetables
asparagus
broccoli
cabbage
carrot
cauliflower
celery
chili
corn
cucumber
eggplant
garlic
green beans
lettuce
mushroom
onion
peas
pepper
potato
tomato
zucchini

Food 1
beans
bread
butter
cereal
cheese
chicken
egg
fish
honey
jam
meat

noodles
nuts
pasta
pepper
rice
salad
salt
soup
spaghetti
sugar

Food 2
chocolate
coffee
cookie
egg roll
french fries
hamburger
ice cream
juice
kebab
milk
pie
pizza
sandwich
soda
sushi
taco
tea
water

Story Time 1
carriage
castle
crown
fairy godmother
flag
king
magic wand
prince
princess
queen
throne
tower

Story Time 2
broom
dragon
dwarf
elf
fairy
flying carpet
forest
genie
giant
knight
magic lamp
sword

treasure chest
witch
wizard

Toys and Games
action figure
blocks
board game
boat
bubbles
coloring book
comic book
computer game
crayons
dice
dinosaur
doll
dollhouse
fire truck
monster
puppet
puzzle
robot
teddy bear
train
yo-yo

Birthday Party
bake
balloon
blow out
bow
cake
candle
candy
card
cupcake
friends
invitation
light
lollipop
popcorn
potato chips
present
wrap
wrapping paper

At the Beach
beach ball
beach chair
cooler
flippers
island
kite
ocean
pail
sailboat
sand

137

ostrich
rhinoceros
spots
stripes
trunk
tusk
zebra

In the Sea
coral reef
crab
dolphin
fin
fish
jellyfish
lobster
mussel
octopus
oyster
pearl
scales
sea horse
seaweed
shark
shrimp
starfish
stingray

turtle
whale

In the Woodlands
beaver
chipmunk
deer
duck
eagle
mouse
nest
pond
rabbit
raccoon
robin
skunk
squirrel
toad
woodpecker

In the Polar Lands
antler
cub
Eskimo
flipper
fox
goose

grizzly bear
igloo
lake
moose
penguin
polar bear
puffin
reindeer
seal
walrus
wolf

In the Desert
cactus
camel
claws
coyote
lizard
oasis
owl
palm tree
rock
sand dune
scorpion
snake
tortoise
vulture

Space
astronaut
constellation
moon
planet
rocket
satellite
space station
spaceship
star
sun
telescope
Mercury
Venus
Earth
Mars
Jupiter
Saturn
Uranus
Neptune

Verbs

bake, **90**
blow out, **90**
brush my teeth, **26**
build, **68**
call my friend, **27**
catch, **46**
chase, **47**
check out, **48**
clap, **97**
clean my room, **27**
climb, **47, 59**
close, **69**
color, **72**
come home, **27**
cook, **28**
cough, **63**
count, **68**
cry, **24**
cut, **73**
dance, **97**
dig, **59, 104**
dive, **107**
do my homework, **27**
draw, **72**
drink, **25**

eat, **25**
eat breakfast, **26**
eat lunch, **26**
eat dinner, **27**
fall, **47**
float, **107**
flush the toilet, **35**
get dressed, **26**
get up, **26**
give, **69**
glue, **73**
go to bed, **27**
go to school, **26**
hammer, **59**
hide, **24**
hop, **46**
hug my dad, **27**
jump, **47**
kick, **47**
kiss my mom, **27**
laugh, **25**
light, **90**
listen, **69**
look at, **68**
make my bed, **26**

measure, **59**
open, **69**
paint, **73, 97**
pass, **54**
plant, **104**
play a guitar, **97**
play with friends, **27**
pour, **54**
pull, **46**
push, **46**
rake, **108**
read, **69**
return, **49**
ride, **46**
ride a bike, **109**
run, **47**
saw, **59**
serve, **54**
sing, **97**
sit down, **69**
skateboard, **109**
sleep, **27**
slide, **46**
smile, **24**
sneeze, **63**

spell, **68**
splash, **107**
stand up, **69**
stir, **54**
sweep, **108**
swim, **107**
swing, **47**
take, **68**
take a bath, **35**
take a picture, **97**
take a shower, **26, 35**
talk, **69**
think, **69**
throw, **47**
wash the dishes, **28**
wash your hands, **35**
watch TV, **27**
water, **104**
wrap, **90**
write, **68**
yawn, **25**
yell, **24**

Letters

Write the letters.

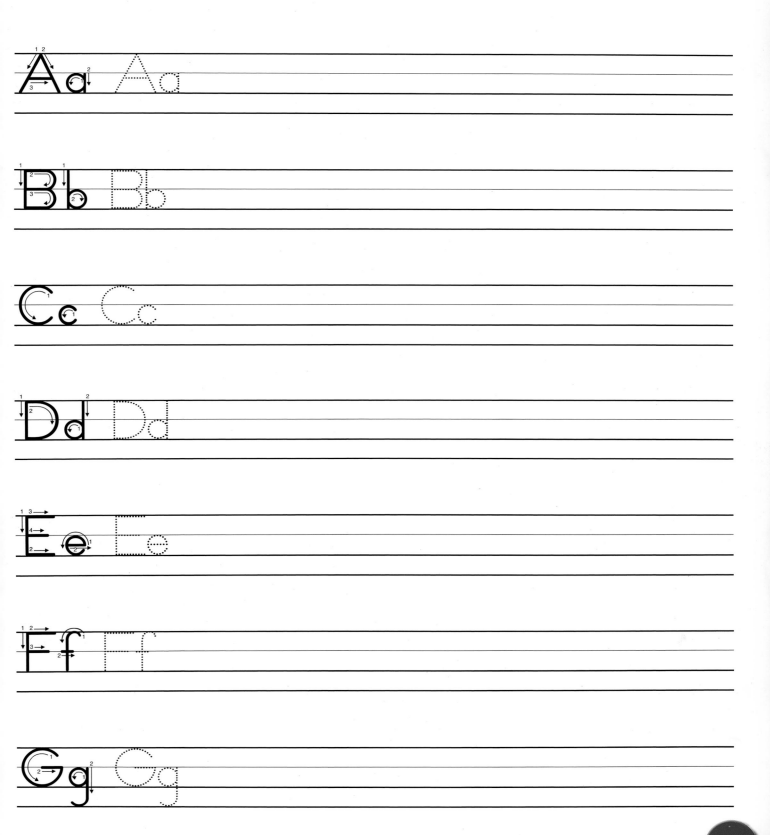

Letters

Write the letters.

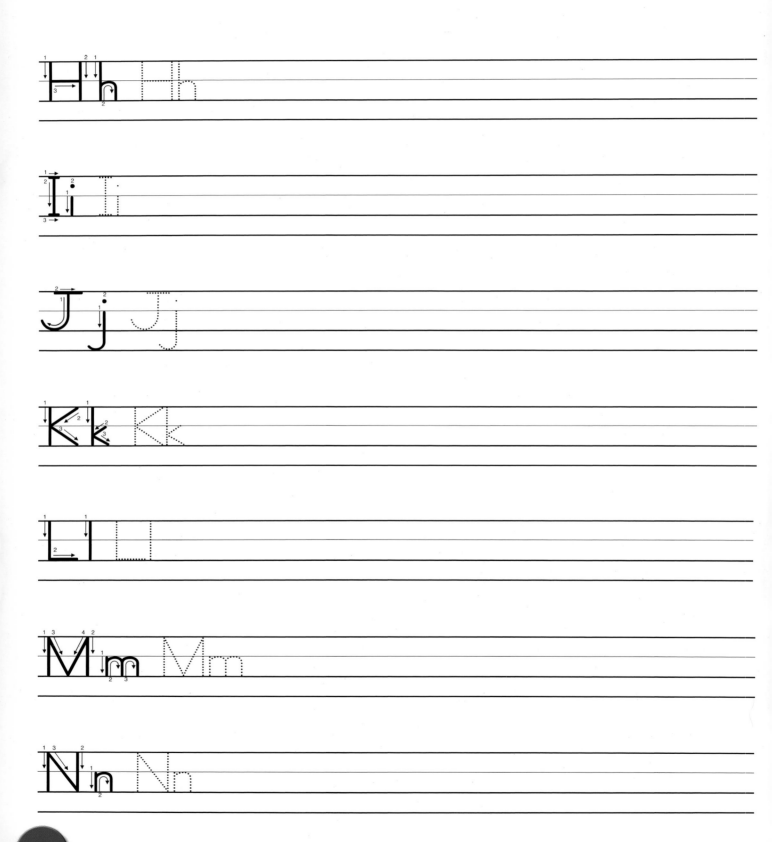

Letters

Write the letters.

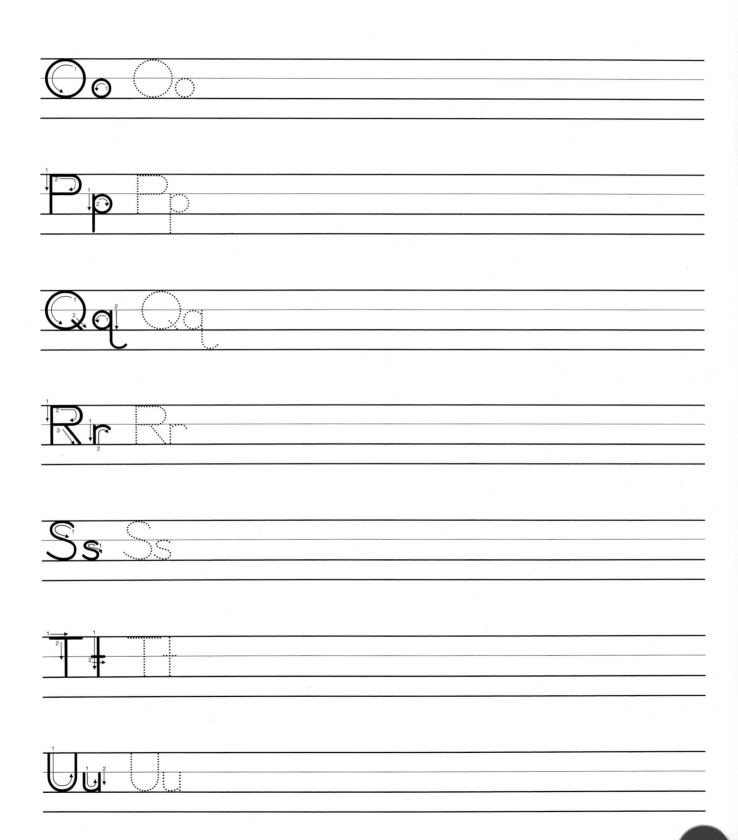

Letters

Write the letters.

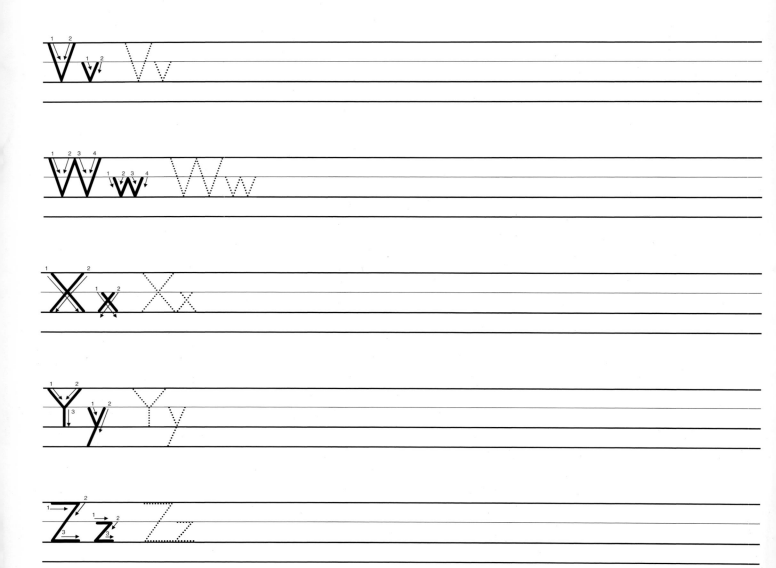

Numbers

Write the numbers.

1 |

2   2

3   3

4   4

5   5

6   6

7   7

8   8

9   9

10   10

11   11

12   12

13   13

14   14

15   15

16   16

17   17

18   18

19   19

20   20

143

Skills Index

Grammar, Usage, and Mechanics

Listening and Speaking

Reading

Vocabulary Development

Credits